BASE JUMPING

Greenwood Guides to Extreme Sports

Surfing: The Ultimate Guide
Douglas Booth

Snowboarding: The Ultimate Guide
Holly Thorpe

BASE JUMPING
The Ultimate Guide

Jason Laurendeau

GREENWOOD GUIDES TO EXTREME SPORTS
Holly Thorpe and Douglas Booth, Series Editors

 GREENWOOD

AN IMPRINT OF ABC-CLIO, LLC
Santa Barbara, California • Denver, Colorado • Oxford, England

Library of Congress Cataloging-in-Publication Data

Laurendeau, Jason.
   Base jumping : the ultimate guide / Jason Laurendeau.
      p. cm. — (Greenwood guides to extreme sports)
   Includes bibliographical references and index.
      ISBN 978–0–313–38397–7 (hardback) — ISBN 978–0–313–38398–4 (e-book)
   1. Extreme sports. 2. Jumping. I. Title.
   GV749.7.L37   2012
   796.04'6—dc23   2012012288

ISBN: 978–0–313–38397–7
EISBN: 978–0–313–38398–4

16 15 14 13 12   1 2 3 4 5

This book is also available on the World Wide Web as an eBook.
Visit www.abc-clio.com for details.

Greenwood
An Imprint of ABC-CLIO, LLC

ABC-CLIO, LLC
130 Cremona Drive, P.O. Box 1911
Santa Barbara, California 93116-1911

This book is printed on acid-free paper ∞

Manufactured in the United States of America

To Carly, Matthew, and Quinn

contents

series foreword

of interest to students and enthusiasts alike, extreme sports are recharging and redefining athletics around the world. While baseball, soccer, and other conventional sports typically involve teams, coaches, and an extensive set of rules, extreme sports more often place the individual in competition against nature, other persons, and themselves. Extreme sports have fewer rules, and coaches are less prominent. These activities are often considered to be more dangerous than conventional sports, and that element of risk adds to their appeal. They are at the cutting edge of sports and are evolving in exciting ways.

While extreme sports are fascinating in their own right, they are also a window on popular culture and contemporary social issues. Extreme sports appeal most to the young, who have the energy and daring to take part in them, and who find in them an alternative culture with its own values and vocabulary. At the same time, surfing and various other extreme sports have long histories and are important to traditional cultures around the world. The extreme versions of these sports sometimes employ enhanced technology or take place under excessively challenging conditions. Thus they build on tradition yet depart from it. Extreme sports are increasingly significant to the media, and corporations recognize the marketing value of sponsoring them. Thus extreme sports become linked with products, their star athletes become celebrities, and their fans are exposed to a range of media messages. Local governments might try to regulate skateboarding and other extreme activities, sometimes out of safety concerns and sometimes out of moral ones. Yet other communities provide funding for skateboard parks, indoor rock climbing facilities, and other venues for extreme sports enthusiasts. Thus extreme sports become part of civil discourse.

Designed for students and general readers, this series of reference books maps the world of extreme sports. Each volume looks at a particular sport and includes information about the sport's history, equipment and techniques, and important players. Volumes are written by professors or other authorities and are informative, entertaining, and engaging. Students using these books learn about sports that interest them and discover more about cultures, history, social issues, and trends. In doing so, they become better prepared to engage in critical assessments of extreme sports in particular and of society in general.

Holly Thorpe and Douglas Booth, Series Editors

preface

I can trace my sociological interest in extreme sports (a contested term) back to a fairly specific moment in my life when my academic interests and my personal passions met. It was the fall of 1996. I was, at the time, enrolled in an undergraduate program in kinesiology, on my way (or so I thought) to doing graduate work in exercise physiology. On the weekends, though, I would put down my books, head out to a local drop zone (sky-diving facility), and do as many jumps as I could fit in and afford before heading back to the city and my next week of classes. As part of my degree program, I was in the process of taking two courses (one in kinesiology and one in sociology) on sociocultural aspects of sport. These courses were opening up a whole new set of research questions that piqued my interest. Around this same time, the most influential instructor in my young skydiving career—Keith—died as a result of a skydiving mishap. I was devastated. I recall spending hours in front of the computer, reading electronic testimonials to Keith's passion, his commitment to the sport and his students, and his zest for life. I literally cried as I read these comments and thought back to my own experiences with Keith, wondering if I ever would have taken up the sport seriously had I not met him. My personal devastation, though, did not, it seemed, shake my resolve to keep jumping. The weekend following Keith's death, I was jumping out of a skyvan (a 19-seat twin-turboprop aircraft) 13,000 feet over a beautiful valley near Kalispell, Montana. And it felt the same. Keith's death, though it had impacted me personally, didn't change my understanding of sky-diving, at least not in a way that I understood at the time.

To my newly developing sociological imagination, this was intriguing. How, I wondered, do people involved in risk sports make sense of the hazards involved? How do they come to terms with the possibility that some of these sports could cost them their lives? Do they embrace risk, manage it, compartmentalize it, or some hybrid of all of the above? Isn't *risk sport* itself a misnomer because it is possible to participate in many of these sports with a good degree of safety (certainly more safety than is generally acknowledged by the public)? (After all, I reasoned, Keith had been doing a particularly hazardous jump when he died.) In short order, I came to find these questions much more compelling than those that I encountered in exercise physiology or elsewhere. My path toward the sociology of sport had been laid out before me. I undertook an M.A. program in sociology, conducting research on skydiving and skydivers. Later, after completing a Ph.D. on an unrelated topic, I returned to my first intellectual love, starting a project on BASE jumping (which, as I'll explain, is related to skydiving in some important ways). This project has occupied much of my attention since I began it in 2007 and forms the foundation for this book.

I drew on a number of research methods as I compiled material for this book. A project on BASE jumping has been on my mind for nearly a decade now, and long before I formally undertook the research, I had numerous conversations with friends who were BASE jumpers about what they did and why they did it. It is perhaps no surprise, then, that the project began with a small number of in-depth interviews with active BASE jumpers. These interviews lasted hours, and in them we discussed jumpers' histories in the sport, their perspectives on risk and danger, the pleasure they took from BASE jumping, and what nonjumpers in their lives thought of their participation. These interviews formed the basis of my initial understandings of the sport, and I still check in with these interviewees from time to time as I'm writing about BASE both to keep them updated on the research and, perhaps more importantly, to get their opinions on the conclusions I draw from the various materials I have gathered over the years.

From the outset of the project, though, I knew I would also want to witness people jumping from bridges, antennae, and other objects in order to better understand both the sport itself and those people involved in it. In the spring of 2007, I began this process of hanging around with jumpers, both while they were doing jumps and while they were socializing at other times. This allowed me to see the day-to-day reality of BASE jumping, witness examples of what I had heard in interviews, and, occasionally, come across something that seemed to contradict what an interviewee had told me. I explored all of these observations, both in the notes I constructed at the end of each day in the field and in numerous informal conversations with a number of jumpers, including some of those I had already interviewed formally. Over the next several months, I spent hundreds of hours with jumpers as they prepared for, undertook, and recounted jumps and as they undertook other, more mundane tasks in the course of their jumping activities. As part of my participant observation of BASE jumping, I have consumed hundreds of videos (e.g., YouTube, amateur, or professionally produced by BASE jumpers), websites (e.g., Blinc, basejumper.com), films (e.g., those produced for the Banff Mountain Film Festival), and other jumping-related materials. Examinations of these materials not only allow me to check what participants have told me, but also point to the complexity of the BASE jumping subculture, provide new directions and questions to explore, and allow me to keep up to speed on new developments and controversies in the sport.

The third main component to this research is that I became, for a time at least, a BASE jumper myself. Especially in light of my previous participation in skydiving, this was a somewhat natural extension of my research project. When one of my interviewees asked me whether I was serious about wanting to do a jump, I barely hesitated. I considered (and consider) my participation in the sport as improving my ability to understand both what it feels like (physically, emotionally, and socially) to parachute from a fixed object and, perhaps more importantly, the ambivalence associated with this participation, at least for some jumpers. Eventually, I decided to use my experiences as important sources of data in and of themselves, engaging in a practice known as autoethnography. By examining my own experiences, and specifically the ways in which they were shaped by (and, in turn, helped constitute) the cultural setting within which they took place, I aim to shed further light on this social world. The idea underlying autoethnography is that a researcher considers her or his personal life, experiences, and emotions, but does so always with one eye on the social context in which these things take place. On the one hand, then, my participation in the sport has put me in a good position to speak to jumpers, as it is clear to them that I have some experience, at least, with the activities, feelings, and perspectives I'm asking them to talk about. On the other hand, it gives me a tremendous amount of insight into both the sport itself and the emotional journey involved, at least at the early stages of involvement. By working back and forth between my feelings and experiences and the cultural influences that shaped them, I am able to arrive at an understanding of the sport and its participants that is more nuanced than that of an outsider who might have less appreciation for the complexities of the experience. I should note that, for some social scientists, this kind of deep involvement threatens to contaminate the objectivity of the researcher. My answer to that (and the answer of many sociologists and autoethnographers) would be fairly straightforward—there is no such thing as objectivity when researching human behavior, especially not human behavior that is as emotionally charged as participation in an activity that participants acknowledge may very well cost them their lives. My approach to this "problem," then, is to acknowledge this up front, identify the factors that shape my approach to and perspectives on the subject, and encourage readers to consider these as they take in my analyses and conclusions.

The final formal method relates specifically to Yosemite National Park (YNP), in California, USA. El Capitan, perhaps the most striking cliff in YNP, is also a critically important site in the history of BASE jumping, for reasons I outline in Chapters 4 and 6. In order to understand the history of the sport of BASE, I knew I had to better understand both this cliff and the activities that took place there, particularly in the late 1970s and early 1980s—the period, it is said, during which the modern version of BASE jumping was born. In order to do so, I accessed archival materials, which were graciously provided by the YNP archives. These materials provided me with a good sense of the number and kinds of jumps being done in YNP at the time and the measures park staff undertook to regulate the activity then known as cliff jumping. I coupled these archival materials with information found in issues of *Parachutist* (a major U.S. skydiving publication) at the time in order to better understand the sometimes contentious relationship between park staff, skydivers, and cliff jumpers (who were, at the time, becoming a group of their own rather than simply a subgroup of skydivers). In addition, one of the archivists suggested I get in touch with two men who were involved in monitoring and policing cliff or BASE jumping during this time and afterwards. Each of these men graciously consented to do a formal interview with me, and these interviews shed light on the events of these years that was not necessarily well captured in the archival materials.

In addition to the formal methods outlined above, as the writing of this book progressed I had a number of informal exchanges with BASE jumpers, especially some of the most experienced and long-term jumpers. This started out as a relatively straightforward effort to make sure I had the facts correct: "Do I have that right? You did your first jump in 1983?" On the whole, though, these jumpers were interested enough in the project, sensing my commitment to getting it "right," that our conversations (electronic or by phone) took on a larger scope. I talked, for example, with Chris "Douggs" McDougall about his philosophy of the sport and the way in which the history of BASE that is often constructed seems to be from a North American perspective. I spoke with Jeb Corliss about the same topic and about the exchanges he routinely has with interviewers who "just plain don't get it," again shedding further light not only on jumpers themselves but on the ways in which they are perceived by the general public, even those who take an interest in BASE for one reason or another. These (and other) conversations contributed both to my understanding of BASE and to my ability to convey the complexities of the sport, its history, and its meaning to those for whom BASE represents their biggest passion (or, as Corliss put it, their reason for being on this earth).

There are only a handful of researchers who have seriously considered the sociological dimensions of extreme sports, and even fewer have conducted in-depth research on skydiving and BASE jumping. And I am, to my knowledge, the only academic who has studied the historical and sociological dimensions of the activity with insider knowledge of the sport, drawn, in my case, both from my years of skydiving and from my brief involvement in BASE. While this may compromise my ability to be objective, it also means that I have a degree of insight into the activity, the culture, and its practitioners that is simply unavailable to outsiders, of whom BASE jumpers tend to be somewhat suspicious. As in the case of practitioners of many of what sociologist Belinda Wheaton (and others) calls lifestyle sports, BASE jumpers tend to be of the opinion that it is impossible to understand BASE without having done it. This is not to suggest that no outsider can understand the activity, but that there are certain dimensions of the activity that were available or understandable to me precisely because of my experience with both skydiving and BASE jumping. I learned a great deal about the sport (sociologically speaking), for example, in the four-day intensive first-jump course I took in the summer of 2007. Not only did I learn the basics of how to BASE jump, but I learned some of the cultural expectations, the ties that bind jumpers together, and the ways that people make sense of injury and death. Having me write a letter to my family explaining that I had died served the course instructor's purposes but also provided me with considerable insight into how jumpers consider and come to terms with the possibility that they might die as a consequence of their participation in BASE. All of the methods described, as well as the kinds of insider knowledge I describe, put me in a perfect position to write this book.

The chapters in this book are organized as follows. In the introductory chapter, I introduce the sport of BASE in a general way. In Chapter 2, I consider some important dimensions of the subculture that has developed around the sport. In Chapter 3, I present an autoethnographic narrative that highlights the emotional intensity of BASE but also the sense in which jumpers' participation may be shaped by commitments and loyalties that lie outside of BASE itself. In Chapter 4, I explore the origins and development of the sport, highlighting the sense in which BASE is related to the idea of human flight as well as its historical connections to sport parachuting (skydiving). I also consider its development as a sport separate from skydiving and new directions (both technological and cultural) in recent years. In Chapter 5, I explain the techniques and equipment of BASE, from the skydiving gear and techniques employed in the earliest jumps of the modern era to the most recent innovations that allow a BASE jumper to fly within inches of cliff faces and tree tops before deploying his or her parachute to land safely. In Chapter 6, I detail a number of important sites and events in BASE, outlining the sense in which some of these have changed or are changing the activity. In Chapter 7, I profile a number of pioneers and icons in BASE, highlighting their contributions to the development of the activity and, in some cases, the ways they have been lionized by mainstream media. In Chapter 8, I conclude with a consideration of future directions for the sport. I point towards the most cutting-edge versions of the activity and the sense in which future directions are difficult to predict in a sport seemingly limited only by the imaginations of those involved in it.

acknowledgments

this book was a labor of love. I have been enthralled by the sport of BASE jumping for nearly a decade and a half now, ever since the peak of my involvement in skydiving. To translate that passion into a text that does the sport and its participants justice, though, involved not only a tremendous amount of time and energy on my part but also the invaluable assistance and support of a number of people.

I would first like to acknowledge the many BASE jumpers who generously shared their time and opinions with me. Whether we talked over email, on the phone, or in person, whether our conversations took place in a coffee shop or on the walk out to an exit, you have made invaluable contributions. Not only have you helped me to understand BASE jumping, but you've reminded me repeatedly what I love about doing research like this—the connections that happen along the way. I'm particularly astonished by, and appreciative of, the jumpers who undoubtedly receive too many interview requests to count and yet responded quickly and graciously to a request from some guy they didn't even know.

Second, my thanks go out to the editors and other authors in this series for their support throughout and for their work, which continues to influence my thinking and writing. Holly Thorpe, in particular, earned my gratitude during the writing of this book for her patience, graciousness, and guidance.

Third, I would like to acknowledge the Yosemite National Park Archives, and the archivists there, without whom a large chunk of the history presented in the chapter on origins and developments would have been missing, incomplete, or even misinformed.

Fourth, my thanks go to the University of Lethbridge and the Social Sciences and Humanities Research Council for providing funding that supported this research project.

Fifth, and finally, I want to acknowledge the tremendous support of my family and friends. I want to especially thank Carly, my partner, for her enthusiasm, support, and love during the process of writing this manuscript. Writing a book (even a small one) takes on a bit of a life of its own—it felt a little bit like I was in a relationship with this book! Carly understood this, helped me find the time and motivation to work on it even when other deadlines were pending, and helped me through those moments when it all felt like too much. Having a partner as loving and supportive as Carly makes me a lucky man indeed. And on top of that, she's an academic herself, so she has an intimate understanding of the joys and pressures of undertaking a project like this.

1. introduction

"3, 2, 1, see ya!" With that, I launched myself from the Perrine Bridge in Twin Falls, Idaho, and began my "career" as a BASE jumper. BASE is an acronym for Building, Antenna, Span (bridge), Earth (cliff). Participants jump from one of these objects (*object* is the general term jumpers use to refer to the fixed object from which they jump) or from one of a number of other fixed objects—such as a silo or a dam—that falls into a general "other" (O) category. At a certain point, a jumper deploys a parachute in order to land safely—in principle at least. The activity only became known as BASE jumping, though, in the early 1980s. In the preceding two decades or thereabouts, it was generally seen as a variant of sky-diving. Cliff-jumping, as it was most often called at the time, was an activity that more daring skydivers took up in order to explore new boundaries in the sport. This period from the mid-1960s to the early 1980s marks the advent of what we might call the modern era of "BASE," as participants call the activity. Earlier still, there are examples of daredevils and adventurers leaping from various fixed objects. For example, Frederick Law jumped from the Statue of Liberty in 1912, a jump I describe in greater detail below. These jumps were generally understood as stunts rather than as a regular form of recreation. We can go back even further, though, to see inventors, pioneers, and daredevils smitten with the idea of human flight. As I argue in Chapter 4, these jumps, in many respects, represent the first steps on the path toward the activity now known as BASE. Jeb Corliss, one of the most well-known contemporary BASE jumpers, put it succinctly: "Were they BASE jumpers? Of course they were!"

Perhaps the first challenge in terms of writing about BASE jumping is deciding what to call it. It is commonly referred to as a sport and is related, as I explain below, to sport parachuting (commonly called skydiving). What's more, with the advent of events like the World BASE Race, there is an element of competition that was previously absent. For some BASE

1

The I. B. Perrine Bridge is approximately 1,500 feet long, spanning Snake River Canyon in Twin Falls, Idaho. Its height (486 feet above Snake River), easy access, and "friendly" (relatively free of obstacles) landing area make the bridge a popular site for neophyte BASE jumpers. (Stephen Griffith/Dreamstime.com)

jumpers, though, calling the activity a sport is something of an insult. For them, there is much more to the activity than chasing around a ball (which is how some of them characterize sports). By contrast, they suggest, BASE jumping is a lifestyle, a spiritual practice of a sort. In this book, then, I'll often use the broader term *activity* to reflect this perspective.

It is worth noting at this early stage that there are a number of different types of BASE jumps. Jumpers launch from different kinds of fixed objects, including, but not limited to, those captured by the BASE acronym. In addition, however, jumpers may vary the kinds of jumps they do in other ways, including the height of the object, the length of delay (if any) prior to activating their parachute, and aerial maneuvers performed, just to name a few. The most important of these variations are explored in the chapters that follow.

In terms of demographics, most BASE jumpers are men, and the age range is generally from the late teens upwards. My observations suggest, though, that the highest concentration of jumpers falls in the late 20s to early 40s. Strictly speaking, there is little to stop someone from simply buying gear and jumping as the activity is not formally regulated. However, jumpers informally regulate who gets started in the sport and what their qualifications are, meaning that most jumpers already have at least a general proficiency in skydiving first. Because skydiving is generally only legal for adults or youth with parental consent, in practice this places something of a lower boundary on the age range of BASE jumpers.

The number of BASE jumpers is rather difficult to pinpoint given the clandestine nature of many jumps; it is in the interests of BASE jumpers not to have the activity too widely publicized. That said, not all BASE jumpers keep their activities to themselves, and BASE has proven to have some cultural cachet, appearing in numerous films, commercials, and other media.

BASE: an extreme activity(?)

Sociologist Deborah Lupton (1999) is one of a number of academics who argue that in recent decades we have seen a fundamental shift in the meanings associated with the term *risk*. It used to be that a risk implied the possibility of a positive outcome or a negative outcome, or the word was used to refer to the likelihood of a natural disaster such as a tornado or hurricane. A "danger" or "hazard," on the other hand, referred to a situation with a strong likelihood of a negative or harmful outcome. Lupton points out that in contemporary society, *risk* has come to be used in much the way *hazard* or *danger* were once employed. Social theorist Ulrich Beck (1992) goes so far as to suggest that we are now in a "risk society." He argues that the very nature of risk has changed in postindustrial societies and that we are fundamentally preoccupied with risk—what he calls the "distribution of bads." In terms of so-called risk sports, sociologist Peter Donnelly (2004) suggests that in contemporary society we are deeply ambivalent about risk, both drawn to and horrified by it. This, he points out, goes some way towards explaining the proliferation of risk sports at the same time as society is increasingly preoccupied with, and anxious about, risks more broadly. This ambivalence is evident in BASE, both in the words of practitioners and in how BASE has been mediated for mass consumption. I offer this all-too-brief discussion of theorizing risk to provide some context for our understanding of contemporary risk sports. Though this is a popular term for sports like skydiving, rock climbing, and hang-gliding, a number of academics (including the authors of books in this series on extreme sports) advocate caution in employing either of these terms. First, as Donnelly (2004) suggests, it is possible to participate in most of these activities with a relatively high degree of safety. Second, terms like *risk sport* and *extreme sport* have, to some extent, been co-opted by corporate interests as these activities have been used to market products, events, and experiences (see, for example, the X Games). In this volume, I will consider the hazards of the sport (and how participants make sense of them) but will endeavor to do so without uncritically assuming that BASE (or any other activity) is an "extreme" sport.

the motivations of BASE jumpers

Many contemporary media representations suggest that BASE jumpers are fearless daredevils with a death wish, and lay perceptions seem to be along the same lines. Research suggests, though, that BASE jumpers are not fearless, nor do they harbor a death wish. Rather, they take up the sport (and continue in it) based in large part on the rewards they receive from participation. In a recent survey of 54 BASE jumpers, Tara Allman and her colleagues (2009) enumerated these benefits. While "risk" and "adrenaline rush" were two of the most often cited benefits, they were not associated with many of the other benefits, several of which are more central and meaningful to participants. These include "personal/spiritual," "sense of belonging," "camaraderie," "sense of accomplishment," and "acquiring a new, elite skill."

This research highlights the many dimensions of BASE jumpers' participation in the activity and the fact that the risks of the sport, for many, play only a small or peripheral role in jumpers' motivations. Similarly, jumpers with whom I have spoken have talked about the dangers of the sport and their related fears, but the fear itself isn't what's valuable for them. Instead, it's the mental and emotional journey upon which they

---

In the 2007 film *20 Seconds of Joy*, director Jens Hoffman explores the motivation of BASE jumpers through the case of Norwegian Karina Hollekim, who ultimately suffers a catastrophic injury. The film won the "Best Film on Mountain Sports" and "People's Choice" awards at the 2007 Banff Mountain Film Festival.

embark as they face that fear. Roger, for example, told me about his first jump. It came at a very difficult point in his life; he found himself at a crossroads of sorts, and as he prepared for his jump he was thinking about these many weighty issues:

> **Roger:** At that point, underneath the bridge, putting my gear on, getting ready and just thinking about . . . it really, and it's one thing that I really love about base jumping . . . every time . . . *puts it in perspective and purges . . . crap from your mind.* It gives me, it gives my brain a good defrag . . . [On the bridge,] . . . I'm thinking about everything, everything, just absolutely everything. Just really strange . . . The video [of the jump] is priceless, it really is. So I show it to everybody and there's just like, cus *nobody's ever seen me like that, you know what I mean? Like this is me, my heart's on my sleeve right now* . . . I can still envision, envision it so well, it's like letting go of that railing and the feeling of that initial . . . It's that first second or so, it was just, I remember because you're up in the steel and you immediately drop below the steel . . .
>
> **Jason:** So what went through your mind in that moment of slow motion, seeing the bridge disappear?
>
> **Roger:** . . . nothing . . . zero! Absolutely nothing, other than what I was feeling or seeing. I wasn't, there was no thought of any of the shit I was thinking about before. There's no thought of, a conscious thought of, okay, I've got to be ready for this, got to be on, you know. It's just, everything stopped, just nothing, yeah.
>
> **Jason:** That was your "defrag"?
>
> **Roger:** Yeah. *By the time I landed ten seconds later I was a different person.*
>
> **Jason:** How so?
>
> **Roger:** Well, the relief, the exhilaration, the, the, working through that fear, just getting over that, the whole lead up.

This excerpt (emphasis added) from the interview with Roger illustrates the sense in which BASE provides him with numerous benefits beyond an "adrenaline rush." For him (and others, as we'll see), BASE is part of spirituality, a search for meaning. His suggestion that he was a "different person" after landing from his first jump clearly illustrates the idea of a search for the self.

I do not present Roger's account to suggest that what BASE means to him is what it means to all jumpers. Past research illustrates that even though a subculture may appear to be relatively undifferentiated from an outsider's position (what sociologist Robert Wood [2003] calls [the appearance of] external cultural stability), in reality there are important differences within the group (in Wood's terms, they are internally highly variable in the extent to which individual members incorporate the values and symbols of the subculture into their own identity). Members of any subgroup such as BASE jumpers, though they may share an understanding of meanings and symbols important to the group, interpret them differently and accord them different levels of importance in light of their own biographies, values, and connections to other people and groups. This, too, will be evident in the coming chapters as I consider the experiences and perspectives of committed, core participants as well as those for whom BASE occupies a less central position.

BASE **jumping and skydiving:** **similarities and differences**

The modern version of BASE owes much to technologies developed in the sport of skydiving; I consider technological dimensions of BASE in more detail in Chapter 5. Despite this degree of overlap, BASE differs from skydiving in some important ways, the most central of which I outline in the coming pages. Much less commercialized than contemporary skydiving, BASE has, to some extent, remained a clandestine activity, not least because many jumps put participants at risk of being arrested on charges such as trespassing or reckless endangerment. At the same time, though, BASE has become a media hit of sorts, appearing in Hollywood and independent films and covered by networks such as ESPN. As jumpers explain, BASE shares a number of technical elements with skydiving, and most BASE jumpers come to the sport with at least a degree of skydiving experience. Despite considerable overlap, the gear used by BASE jumpers is somewhat different from skydiving equipment. Unlike skydiving rigs (see Laurendeau 2006), most BASE rigs do not have a reserve parachute. In skydiving, if you experience a malfunction of your "main" (main parachute), you can generally rely on your "reserve." While skydivers pack their own mains (with greater or lesser degrees of care), only a certified expert (called a rigger) is authorized to pack reserves. Reserves must be carefully inspected and repacked regularly regardless of whether or not they have been used. In the event that they are needed, of course, they absolutely must work. BASE jumpers suggest that the principal reason for the absence of a reserve on a BASE rig is to keep the equipment as simple and straightforward as possible; the idea is that fewer components make for fewer potential problems. Also, many jumps are made from a low enough altitude that there simply would not be time to deploy a reserve parachute. It is in this sense that jumpers sometimes refer to their one and only parachute as their reserve. It has to work every time. The corollary to that is that BASE jumpers tend to exercise much more care in packing than do most skydivers.

Another important difference between the two activities is that insiders and outsiders share the perspective that BASE is significantly more hazardous than skydiving. While many so-called risk sports can be undertaken with a relatively high degree of safety, this claim seems more difficult to make with respect to BASE (acknowledging, of course, that what constitutes a relatively high degree of safety is a matter of subjective interpretation). One informant suggested that if 95 percent of the general population think that skydiving is crazy, 95 percent of skydivers think that BASE is crazy. When I've shared this observation with other BASE jumpers, it seems to ring true. In addition to these anecdotal observations, recent articles in the *British Journal of Sports Medicine* (Westman et al. 2008) and the *New Zealand Medical Journal* (Monasterio and Mei-Dan 2008) offer further evidence (in one case based on a small sample of current BASE jumpers, in the other based on an analysis of documented BASE fatalities) that BASE is significantly more hazardous than skydiving. Still, expressed in terms of probabilities, BASE is perhaps less risky than laypeople might think. Based on an analysis of over 20,000 jumps from a peak in Norway, three health studies researchers concluded that approximately 0.04 percent (1 in 2,317) of all jumps end in fatality, and approximately 0.4 percent (1 in 254 jumps) result in a nonfatal injury (Soreide, Ellingsen, and Knutson 2007).

There are several factors that contribute to what jumpers acknowledge to be the high level of danger in the activity. First, BASE is often undertaken from such a low altitude—sometimes as low as 100 or 200 feet—that if something goes wrong there is little time to recover. Several of my contacts, for example, have experienced an equipment malfunction of some kind and been injured as a result of landing without a fully inflated parachute. Two of these jumpers required emergency surgery and extensive rehabilitation to recover from their injuries.

Second, landing areas for BASE are often small or filled with hazards. As Roger put it, "You've got shit everywhere and boulders and landing areas that are far away." At the Perrine Bridge in Idaho (often simply called "the Perrine"), for instance, as part of preparing me for my first jump, another jumper outlined the features of the landing area (a very forgiving one, by BASE standards). After pointing out where I should land, this jumper specifically admonished me to "stay north of the death line." South of that line, he explained, there are all sorts of huge boulders. Worse still, they're somewhat hidden by the grass, so you don't see them until it is too late to do anything about it. The fact that jumpers refer to this as the "death line" illustrates both the seriousness of the hazards and jumpers' awareness of the very real consequences of misjudgments. Though the term "death line" may be invoked with a degree of humor, it is quite clear that the message itself is extremely serious.

Third, unlike skydiving, there is often a serious possibility of "object strike"—hitting the object from which one has just launched, either in freefall or under canopy. In the course of my investigation of BASE, I met three people who had experienced object strike (one ended up stranded overnight on a cliff face in the freezing cold while a highly technical rescue operation was mounted) and heard numerous other secondhand stories of object strike. For many jumpers, object strike represents perhaps the greatest hazard in the activity. This possibility makes it extremely important that jumpers maintain their heading as they launch from an object, that they stay clear of the object in freefall (this is particularly evident in "proximity flying"), and that their parachute opens on heading. One jumper sent me a video of a jump from a cliff, one with which he is very familiar. On this particular jump, though, his launch happened to be slightly off heading to the right (perhaps 30°), and then his parachute opened off heading as well (approximately 90° right). Because parachutes generate forward speed as they open (as I explain in Chapter 5), his flew him directly into the face of the cliff from which he had just launched. He was able to recover and landed without injury. Nevertheless, this illustrates the potential dangers of object strike.

One particularly telling difference between BASE and skydiving can be found in how participants talk about the hazards of the sport. In the case of skydiving, many (though by no means all) jumpers suggest that the sport is not particularly dangerous. They believe that they can make smart choices about what kinds of jumps to do, under what conditions, and with what equipment, and can keep themselves safe (Laurendeau 2006). While the majority of skydivers downplay the hazards of the sport, BASE jumpers, on the whole, are much more sober in their assessment of their chosen form of recreation. They acknowledge that there is a much smaller margin for error in BASE than in skydiving and that they are very likely to be injured (perhaps seriously injured or even killed) as a result of their participation. This assessment is evident not only in conversations with and between jumpers but also in formal training environments.

One salient example of BASE jumpers' assessments of the hazards of the activity is found in their perspectives on the possibility of being killed as a result of their participation in BASE. Most of the jumpers I've met have considered the possibility of being killed and have come to terms with it. The general perspective seems to be along the lines of "I'd rather do the things I love, even knowing that they may kill me, than live a life where I'm not being true to my passions." There is more to it than that, as we'll see in the coming pages, but suffice it to say that jumpers take the hazards of the activity quite seriously. They go to great lengths to ensure that their jumps are "repeatable"—that is, that they live to jump another day. In fact, two French researchers have referred to BASE as the "most serious play in the world." That said, a number of jumpers experience some ambivalence as they negotiate their participation in the sport. This is something I explore in Chapter 3, and in more detail in the autoethnographic paper upon which it is based (Laurendeau 2011). In addition, though, it is captured in conversations, discussion board threads, and other media. It is not simply that jumpers believe they won't be hurt or killed, or don't care about this possibility. Rather, they generally acknowledge this possibility and feel quite strongly about it. They feel just as much conviction, though, about their reasons for continuing to take part in the activity.

In order to participate in this sport with the greatest degree of safety possible (while still "pushing the envelope"), jumpers spend a great deal of time and energy making sure that they are doing the things they need to do in order for jumps to go well. Whether in online discussions or in person, for example, jumpers go to great lengths to share information about things that are working well for them (such as a particular packing technique) as well as things that have gone wrong. This practice is aimed at sharing information with one another so that jumpers can learn from each other's experiences and hopefully be safer as a result. They also spend tremendous amounts of time carefully considering jumps they are about to do (or are deciding whether or not to do). This is evident, to some extent, even in a situation where they are jumping a relatively simple object with which they are familiar. At the Perrine, for example, I have watched jumpers spend half an hour or more evaluating wind conditions, changing weather patterns, and similar factors as they evaluate a (potential) jump. In the case of jumps that are more complicated, this phenomenon is even more striking. Early in my fieldwork, I witnessed a group of four highly experienced jumpers spend 20 very serious minutes in almost total silence as each of them evaluated a cliff jump. Though they collaboratively discussed elements of the jump, the cliff itself, and the potential landing areas, they then each decided individually whether or not they were willing to jump. In my fieldnotes, I wrote:

> Small group of experienced jumpers, by invite only. After evaluating the jump, James decided not to go. He thought it looked a bit technical, and wasn't feeling quite current enough on "runners." Kevin didn't say a word about James' decision (neither did the other two). When I asked Kevin about it afterwards, he explained that this was a "real" BASE jump (unlike the bridge, he implied), and "it takes more balls" to stand down than to jump. (May 2007)

This situation illustrates both how carefully jumpers consider their abilities to "handle" particular jumps and the sense in which these decisions are embedded in (sub)cultural relations in BASE (something I consider in more depth in Chapter 2).

The benefits I mention above are, perhaps, a bit difficult for many nonjumpers to understand and even for some jumpers to articulate. In the simplest terms, the activity provides a thrill that jumpers are unable to experience or create through other activities. Even this, however, is a tremendous oversimplification. If the activity was little more than a search for thrills, jumpers could accomplish this in a myriad of other ways, including activities with much better records of safety. They could go on rollercoaster rides, for example. Two things are critical to understand, however, in order to make sense of why jumpers would rather leap from a cliff than strap themselves into a carnival ride. The first of these is that part of the allure of BASE is that it is a demanding activity. The draw is not simply the thrill but is also at a fundamental level about the thrill of taking on an activity that requires a high level of skill and that would frighten most people to the point that they would not be able to function properly. To look fear in the face and still do all of the things you have to do to BASE jump safely is tremendously demanding and provides a sense of satisfaction for a great number of jumpers. Sociologist Stephen Lyng (1990; 2005) refers to this as edgework. He suggests that people engaged in these activities discover or experience their "true" selves as they negotiate the boundaries between "chaos and order," "sanity and insanity," even "life and death."

Second, for many jumpers, BASE serves as a vehicle for a spirituality of sorts. I don't mean to suggest that it is an organized religion of any kind. Instead, a number of jumpers consider their participation in the sport to be an avenue of exploring themselves or their relationship with greater powers, however they might understand that idea. For many jumpers, freefalling along a sheer cliff face at upwards of 100 km/h allows them to know both themselves and the world of which they are a part in a deeper, more meaningful way than they might otherwise be able to achieve.

Based on the description I've offered of a general approach to safety, it may seem somewhat paradoxical that jumpers continually test themselves against new, more technical, and more challenging jumps of various kinds. A skydiving informant once told me that skydiving could be incredibly safe if everyone jumped with large, very forgiving canopies (jumpers sometimes use *canopy* to refer specifically to the parachute itself—the wing-like structure without the suspension lines) and landed them in the middle of huge fields with no obstacles. However, he said, "that wouldn't be any fun!" The same phenomenon is evident—to an even greater degree—in BASE jumping. Part of the allure is not simply to take risks for the sake of taking risks. Instead, the idea is to exercise skill and good judgment in order to determine what constitutes a reasonable level of risk, taking into consideration such things as one's level of experience and skill, weather conditions, and so on. So to the experienced BASE jumper, a jump from the 486 foot Perrine Bridge, with a big, open landing area and plenty of "outs," might be boring. (An out is a safe landing area in the event that you can't safely reach your "plan A" landing area. In the case of the Perrine, you can almost always land in the water if all else fails, an idea referenced in the adage "clothes dry faster than bones heal.") Numerous jumpers, in fact, use a trip to Idaho to get in a number of jumps and get themselves "current" (you are considered current if you have done a number of jumps recently) after a layoff from BASE. If they have not jumped over the winter, for example, they use these "simple" jumps to refamiliarize themselves with their gear, jumping techniques, and, just as importantly, the emotional dimensions of BASE before engaging in more challenging jumps. It may seem paradoxical to a nonjumper that a BASE jump can be boring. Lyng's notion of edgework is again helpful here. In both skydiving and BASE (as well as other edgework activities), the "edge" is fluid and contingent. Each jumper's edge is different from that of other jumpers and shifts as he or she gains experience, expertise, and judgment. My first BASE jump, for example, had me "crowding the edge," in Lyng's terms, overwhelmed with emotion and excitement. An experienced and current jumper, however, would likely have found the same jump rather unsatisfying.

In order to keep BASE jumps exciting and interesting, then, most jumpers continually seek out new challenges and experiences. They might jump from different or lower objects, engage in more technical launches, or find other ways to expand their skills and experiences. In so doing, they keep individual jumps entertaining while also shifting the edge for themselves. Perhaps the most technically demanding dimension of the sport, currently, is the employment of wingsuit technology. Jumpers wear a suit designed to slow their fall rate (vertical rate of descent) and increase their ability to generate horizontal speed. This allows a practiced wingsuit flyer to spend a long time in freefall, flying within inches of cliff faces, tree tops, and other obstacles in an activity known as proximity flying. I consider wingsuit BASE and proximity flying in greater detail in Chapters 5 and 8, in particular.

2. BASE culture, BASE ethics

building on the introductory chapter, I continue here to explore the ways BASE jumpers make sense of their participation in the activity. I do so, however, with an eye towards the group context from within which they engage in this process. My aim is to outline the extent to which this sense-making is a fundamentally social activity. Though we often hear individual explanations for participation in so-called risk sports, I highlight the sense in which we can (and should) understand this as a collective process as well as an individual one. In order to do so, I outline some of the distinguishing qualities of what sociologist Robert Stebbins (2007) calls "serious leisure." I then consider what sociologists of sport have had to say about subculture theorizing and what light this helps us shed on BASE at the group level. In particular, I consider the "do it yourself" ethos evident in BASE and explain how we can understand the construction of risk as part of a *collective* sense-making activity.

One of the elements of BASE that makes it difficult to outline the culture of the activity is that it has undergone dramatic changes over the course of the last three decades—essentially its entire modern history. To be sure, the technology associated with BASE has changed substantially, as I describe in greater detail in Chapter 5. In addition, though, the broader culture of the sport has been transformed by the rapid increase in the ability to share information widely. The advent of the Internet has meant that information that used to travel more or less by word of mouth—when someone had "opened" a new object, for example—is now sometimes globally available hours (even minutes) after the event has taken place. Jeff Ferrell, Stephen Lyng, and Dragan Milovanovic (2001), in fact, have suggested that one central feature of the BASE community is what they call the "elongation of meaning"—the extent to which jumpers film their exploits and then relive them later as they and others watch these videos. To some of the "old guard," this rapid dissemination of information means that newer jumpers don't necessarily approach BASE with as much patience as did jumpers in the "early years." They worry that new jumpers will try to accomplish too much too soon rather than slowly developing sets of skills and experiences.

BASE jumping as a form of serious leisure

Robert Stebbins's (2007) concept of serious leisure has proven to have tremendous influence over the last two decades. Not only has this allowed researchers to better understand and categorize leisure activities, but it has provided them with analytical tools to explore numerous dimensions of these activities and the perspectives of those who take them up. Stebbins (2007, 11–12, emphasis in original) outlines six distinguishing qualities of serious leisure: (1) the "occasional need to *persevere*"; (2) finding "a leisure *career* in the endeavour"; (3) significant effort employing "specially acquired *knowledge, training, experience,* or *skill*"; (4) participants receive "*durable benefits*" from their involvement; (5) a "*unique ethos*" develops for participants in a particular form of serious leisure; and (6) participants "tend to *identify* strongly with their chosen pursuits." Stebbins points out that the serious leisure endeavor is shaped "by its own special contingencies, turning points and stages of achievement or involvement" (2007, 11). The notion of serious leisure is helpful for this discussion of BASE for two main reasons. First, it helps illustrate the place BASE occupies in the lives of practitioners and the idea that jumpers have a "career" in the activity. Second, it provides a framework within which we can explore the sense in which the "contingencies" and "turning points" Stebbins describes are shaped by *social* processes.

As Stebbins (2007) explains, there is a variety of forms of serious leisure. BASE falls into the category of a "hobbyist activity," as it is an amateur pursuit without a professional counterpart. This is not to suggest that *no* BASE jumpers endeavor to earn material rewards through BASE jumping; a select few are in a position to do so through avenues such as corporate sponsorship or instruction. Another way jumpers parlay their expertise into (semi-)professional careers is through film making, including both films produced primarily for other BASE jumpers and those targeting a broader audience, such as those produced for the Banff Mountain Film Festival. In addition, the development of certain BASE competitions (including the World BASE Race, which I detail in Chapter 6) point towards the possibility, at least, of professionalism coming about in this way. In light of the spiritual orientation of some jumpers, not to mention the interests of many in keeping BASE out of the limelight, each of these activities has stirred up some degree of controversy in the BASE community.

To return to Stebbins's six distinguishing qualities, I will briefly outline the sense in which BASE meets each criterion. Without question, jumpers occasionally need to persevere in their activity, as illustrated by an interviewee who broke his back on a jump and had to endure months of sometimes frustrating physical therapy before returning to jump. Eventually, he returned to BASE, overcoming dramatic odds in order to do so. His return took place during my time in the field, and it was quite something to witness both his excitement and his fear prior to this jump. Both may have been heightened due to the fact that his first jump back was at the site of the jump that resulted in his injury. "I think I'm going to pee myself," he joked as he arrived at the bridge. Once he got over this initial apprehension, however, he reveled in his return to BASE that week. Similarly, jumpers engage in a leisure career, advancing through various stages of expertise and achievement in the activity. Jumpers begin their careers by learning the basic skills and sets of knowledge in one of two main ways that I consider in greater detail later in the chapter. They then proceed to acquire more advanced physical skills as well as a body of experiences that help them make choices about what kinds of jumps to do and under what conditions to do them. This is not to suggest that this is a linear process. Jumpers sometimes pause their careers, for example, before taking them up again. As Michael explained, "People have stopped base jumping for a couple of years and then have said, 'Ah, actually, you know, I'm back into it now.' "

Without a doubt, jumpers expend considerable effort acquiring the skills, technical knowledge, and training to engage in the "most serious play in the world." As I mentioned above, they devote considerable time and resources (some of it during their careers as skydivers) simply in order to establish the skills and awareness to undertake the most basic of BASE jumps. From there, it can take several years and hundreds of jumps before they would be considered (or consider themselves) expert. This acquisition of skills and knowledge happens in a number of ways. Whether through formal training environments, informal conversations, online resources, or other methods, jumpers continue to refine their skills and add to their experiences as their careers proceed. As mentioned in Chapter 1, for many jumpers this sets the stage for them to explore "the edge" in different and more challenging ways.

The "unique ethos" of BASE is immediately evident in the shared practices, beliefs, and perspectives in the community. This is not to suggest that all jumpers approach the sport or understand their involvement in the same way. Despite individual and within-group variations, though, a set of shared meanings is evident. BASE jumpers tend to identify very strongly with the pursuit, spending enormous amounts of time and money on BASE, planning travel around jumps they would like to do, and often counting other BASE jumpers among their closest friends. One of the many ways this identification is evident is through social networking sites such as Facebook. Even a cursory glance at the Facebook sites of BASE jumpers (their friends, likes, photos, status updates, and so on) reveals the centrality of BASE in the lives of many, if not most, jumpers.

BASE (sub)culture

In the simplest terms, sociologists talk about subcultures as subgroups organized around particular values, beliefs, practices, and worldviews. Crosset and Beal (1997) have argued, though, that there is a risk of this term being used so broadly as to be meaningless. As they point out, the worldview of subcultures tends to be one that opposes the mainstream in some important ways. Beal (1996) and others have elaborated on this idea, suggesting that although subcultures are organized around oppositional values, they often reproduce the status quo in certain ways as well. One of the values central to the subcultures of a number of alternative sports is an emphasis on self-regulation and self-determination. Participants in these activities suggest that mainstream sporting activities are overly commodified and regulated, and set out to organize themselves in opposition to this model. This is clearly evident in the do-it-yourself (DIY) ethos in BASE. Moreover, this ethos is intertwined with the subcultural construction of risk. Sociologist Lisa McDermott (2007) suggests that, at a macro level, risk performs particular functions socially, culturally, and politically. I and others have pointed out that the same is true in more micro-level interactions taking place among participants in so-called risk sports. Whether, how, and the extent to which participants individually and collectively construct and negotiate risk tells us something about both the individuals that take up activities like BASE and also the subcultures that form around these activities. In this section, then, I outline the DIY ethos in BASE and its connections to the ways jumpers make sense of the hazards of the sport.

To begin, it is worth reiterating that jumpers take the hazards of the sport very seriously. As Michael put it:

> Well, I mean the price is that this is, extremely dangerous, you know? . . . Even from something safe like the Perrine . . . When everything goes wrong, um, it's still 6 seconds from the top to the bottom and it, it just goes by really really fast . . . [so] you need to be aware of the fact that these, that things can go wrong, and that they can go wrong in ways that you could never imagine if you were . . . skydiving.

When asked about their involvement in BASE, many jumpers talk about a risk/reward ratio. The risks are high, they suggest, but the rewards are even higher. Recall from the introductory chapter that those rewards include mastery of difficult skills, camaraderie, and many others (Allman et al. 2009). One of the attractions of the sport not discussed by Allman and her colleagues is the DIY attitude that pervades the activity. In contrast to skydiving, for example, jumpers do not rely on an airplane to get them "to altitude" (in skydiving terms). Instead, they most often hike or climb their way to the "exit" in order to jump. In addition, BASE jumpers are generally much more knowledgeable about, and involved with, their equipment than the average skydiver. Belinda Wheaton (2004) argues that this DIY ethos is increasingly evident in what she calls "lifestyle sports." She and others locate this ethos within the discourse of neoliberalism that valorizes individual management of risk profiles and individualizes responsibility for risk taking.

In addition to the practical elements of the activity (e.g., that jumpers don't rely on airplanes), this DIY ethos is evident in the discursive construction of BASE as an unregulated activity. Jumpers, it is said, are responsible for their own safety (and everything that entails), and no one tells them how to do so. This is a topic of ongoing discussion, as illustrated by a 2007 thread on a popular website devoted to BASE, an excerpt of which follows:

> —Would you support a BASE Governing Body and only perform jumps according to the rules set forth by the BASE Governing Body?
> —Butters
> —didn't [sic] even read the message, saw the title and voted.
> —BASE is not illegal! Trespassing is and private property will never be given rights to in the US, this country is too sue happy. An Antenna or Building owner would not allow jumping in risk of a lawsuit from the jumper or others due to death or property damage.

BASE jumper leaping from the New River Gorge Bridge in West Virginia.
(iStockPhoto.com)

—...I would tell a BASE Governing Body to go to hell if they told me not to trespass anymore and can only jump in [Twin Falls], Moab or the likes around the world. It's just unnecessary...
—I joined BASE for the freedom,

> I don't listen to the rules set by the government, police. NPS ect.
>   [*sic*] why would I be interested in yours?
> What are you going to do?
> Hang out at objects and check my log book before you let me jump.
> I jump my objects
> When I want
> My way
> That is BASE for me................ ....
> Greeny
> —Go skydiving Butters
> (http://www.BASEjumper.com/cgi-bin/forum/gforum.cgi?post=2728327;#2728327, accessed May 5, 2010)

While some contributors to the above forum expressed support for the idea of a BASE governing body, they were outnumbered by a margin of roughly 10 to 1 by those who (sometimes vehemently) opposed this idea. As Roger explained in an interview, this is, in part, rooted in the history of BASE:

> Because it's not like skydiving where you've got drop zones here, here and here and they already have to follow these fairly strict transportation laws because there's aircraft involved. ... Whereas, BASE-jumping was born out of you know, like they say, racing the Jolly Roger and giving your middle-finger-salute. Like that's the way BASE [was] kind of born.

In his interview, Matthew elaborated on this idea, highlighting the general ethos in BASE that jumpers should be self-regulating:

> I don't think it should be regulated at all. Um, in all honesty, it's one of the attractions I have to the thing is, with anything, people tell you, here are the rules, you can ... take skydiving, here are the rules but

you're not allowed to do a two-way with friends. You're only allowed to do a two-way if you have an A and your buddy has a B and a hundred jumps and blah, blah, blah . . . that's why I think BASE jumping and really the heart and core BASE jumping is ultimately, you can do what you want.

Roger and Matthew are by no means the only jumpers to suggest that BASE has a history as a renegade activity. This particular "history" of BASE, though, seems to be a selective and partial one, one that seems to romanticize the early years of the activity in certain respects. As I delve into in greater depth in Chapter 4, the early history of BASE does not necessarily paint a clear picture of BASE as a renegade activity (or all participants as renegades). Indeed, this is related to the argument that subcultures often position themselves as oppositional even though they reproduce the status quo in certain ways. It may very well be, then, that this imagined history fits nicely with this positioning, helping to construct BASE as an activity that arose, in part at least, as a form of resistance. As we will see in Chapter 4, the National Park Service was understood to represent all that BASE jumpers (then called cliff jumpers) stood against, and yet there was a brief period of a fair degree of cooperation between advocates of this nascent activity and the powers they ostensibly opposed.

The ethos of jumpers choosing their own "path" (as a couple of interviewees called it) in BASE, and encouraging others to do so as well, is also evident in the ways jumpers respond to each other's choices. For example, numerous jumpers pointed out that even if someone is doing something they think is unwise, they generally won't "stick their noses in there" (for a discussion of formal and informal regulation in skydiving, see Laurendeau and Gibbs Van Brunschot 2006). Similarly, jumpers emphasize that there is no pressure to do a particular jump; people generally support others who choose to "stand down." Recall the story presented in the previous chapter of James standing down from a cliff jump. Earlier, Kevin (who was with James at the cliff) had been pressuring another jumper at a nearby (and relatively safe) bridge to do particular jumps. I wondered about this, as numerous jumpers had told me in interviews that this kind of pressure was extremely uncommon. Others suggested that this was just "Kevin being Kevin," that he wasn't *really* pressuring this jumper. When he didn't say anything about James's decision to stand down at the cliff, I took the opportunity to clarify. Recall his response to my query. He suggested that this was a *real* BASE jump, and that it "takes more balls" to stand down than to jump. This illustrates two important ideas. First, it points to the kinds of judgments participants make about what constitutes authentic involvement in a given activity (see Hunt 1995). Second, it highlights the importance of the idea that jumpers manage their own choices as they engage in the activity. At one and the same time, then, we see individual decision making emphasized but also an emphasis on the group context (shared meanings, expectations) within which jumpers make these choices. Both the individual and group levels are again visible in the following excerpt from my interview with Michael:

> And, walking away [deciding not to jump] is, is reasonably easy when you're at the exit point and then when you're about 10 minutes/ 15 minutes away from the exit point, you [may think], "Oh man, I'm such a candy ass! I can't believe I just stepped away. You know maybe, maybe, if I weren't you know, doubting myself, maybe [if] I were, I don't know, a jumper with balls or something, that I would have, ah, that I would have done that." . . . prior to really talking to a lot of people, it seems like everybody else are these hard-core jumpers who always do whatever. And then you talk to these people, and you're like, "Holy Crap." Everybody's scared and everybody walks down.

Michael's words here are instructive. They provide us with insight into the individual decision-making process—how jumpers make sense of (or don't make sense of) particular jumps. In addition, though, they point to the importance of the sense-making processes of others. Recall that I mentioned jumpers sharing information about packing, gear, and so on. They also, however, share subcultural stores of knowledge about making sense of hazards, the benefits of participation, and what constitutes acceptable risk.

In terms of the DIY ethos outlined above, jumpers clearly position BASE in contrast to other recreational activities in their emphasis on its supposed roots as a rebel activity. They specifically compare it to skydiving, pointing out that there are no rules in BASE as there are in skydiving. It is also contrasted with mainstream sports in that BASE jumpers suggest it is something much bigger—akin to a spiritual practice. In these ways, jumpers position BASE as a countercultural practice of sorts, emphasizing its uniqueness. Despite this DIY ethos, though, there are ways in which we see jumpers' activities regulated. Their "careers" in BASE are shaped, to some extent, by the esteem in which other jumpers hold them and by their adherence to a set of informal expectations known as "BASE ethics." So while BASE is generally not formally regulated, there are informal mechanisms for exercising social control over (potential) jumpers' careers. Broadly speaking, jumpers act as gatekeepers towards both prospective and current jumpers. This happens in two main ways, which I will consider in the sections the follow.

getting started

When one is thinking about getting started in BASE, it is not as simple as in the case of some other extreme sports. One does not walk off the street, find an expert certified in BASE, and pay him or her to provide a thrilling, but more or less safe, initiation to the activity (see Palmer 2002). Instead, one must generally find an "in" of some kind. This often involves expressing interest to a current BASE jumper. Here is the first place we see some kind of social control in operation, as outlined in this excerpt from an interview with Michael:

> **Jason:**   . . . what do you do when somebody says, you know, "I'd really like to get into that!"
>
> **Michael:**   Ah! I think that's like uh, you know, I think that's like somebody starting undergrad at university and saying, "I'd really like to get into brain surgery." Um, in that, you're so far away from being able to make that choice that, that in my opinion, you don't even know who you're going to be when you're actually presented with that opportunity. And so especially when somebody with no skydiving experiencing at all says, "Wow, I'd really to do that!" . . . what I do is I . . . say, you know, "Here's a drop zone that's local. Go on out there, enjoy yourself. Get a few hundred jumps under your belt and don't worry about BASE." You know?

Even in the case of prospective BASE jumpers *with* some skydiving experience, current jumpers are somewhat wary, looking for particular skills and experiences before they are willing to help someone get started in BASE. As Roger put it,

> There's something, I think, that counts for a lot, I would rather help out somebody who say, has three hundred skydives but has been around

the sport for eight years or known people than somebody who's done
two hundred jumps in the last six months and wants to get into BASE.
Because [those who haven't "been around" long] haven't seen a femur
sticking out of a leg yet. They haven't seen a friend die. They haven't
had their friends get injured.

As outlined in these interview excerpts, current jumpers have particular
criteria that they keep in mind when deciding whether and how to mentor
prospective jumpers. For one thing, they are concerned that prospective
jumpers genuinely understand what they are getting themselves into. For
another, they are looking for a particular set of skills and awareness, especially "under canopy" (as opposed to in freefall). Matthew, for example,
described his initial efforts at convincing a BASE jumper to mentor him:
"I knew I needed to learn accuracy [a discipline involving landing as close
as possible to a target], I needed to learn canopy control. Like, he just said,
'I'm not even really gonna pay attention to you until you seriously start
doing this stuff.' So that's what I did. . . . " In time, Matthew convinced
this jumper that he was serious about learning the sport and hung around
for two years learning about the sport before doing his first BASE jump:

So I learned, I learned a ton over those two years. Just how it went.
I did maybe, what I could afford for skydives, fifty or sixty a season.
Which isn't a lot. But the whole time I was doing it, he was teaching me
accuracy, um, obstacle avoidance drills. So, practicing if I were
opening during a skydive, pretending like there's something right in
front of me, trying to get turned around 180 degrees as quickly as
possible and all these sorts of things.

Eventually, Matthew undertook his first jump at Bridge Day and is now a
committed BASE jumper at a more advanced stage of his leisure career.
His mentor, though, did little to encourage Matthew until he was convinced that Matthew possessed the right skills, motivation, and attitude
to proceed.

In recent years, a more institutionalized alternative has emerged for
new jumpers. A small number of experienced jumpers and equipment
manufacturers now offer first-jump courses for prospective jumpers.
Here, too, we see gatekeepers taking very seriously whether a prospective
jumper really understands the hazards of the sport. This was illustrated
when, on the first day of *my* first jump course, my instructor (Cam) had
me write a letter to my family explaining that I had died doing a BASE

jump. Cam explained that this letter—which he has all of his students write—serves two purposes. First, it provides some measure of insurance against a jumper's family suing him or someone else in the BASE community; he specifically instructs jumpers to ask their loved ones not to hold other jumpers accountable for their deaths. Second, though, he has jumpers write this at the outset of the course to ensure that they understand the hazards of the sport and the reality that it could cost them their lives.

It is also important, though, that prospective jumpers are believed to have good judgment. When I was considering applying for the first-jump course, for example, a contact explained that my skydiving experience as a coach and instructor would make me an "attractive candidate" even though I hadn't been an active skydiver for several years. As Michael explained, the community is so small and tightly-knit that word travels quickly:

> [A local jumper] had planned to take the [first-jump] course . . . and one of the other jumpers in fact, called up the manufacturer who they were doing the course from, or who was giving the course and said, "There's no way this guy should be near a first jump course." Which I thought was a bit of a rash decision but I've contacted the people myself . . . Because originally they had sort of just blacklisted him from the course for a while . . . even the sort of commercial courses, such as they are, or whatever, are interested in that sort of thing and a BASE jumper calls them up and says, "Hey, this guy does not belong in your course." Then you will never get into a course. . . . Nobody wants to, you know, nobody wants to toss an uncontrolled jumper in with a bunch of their buddies.

Here, again, we see the sense in which jumpers' (or prospective jumpers') leisure careers hinge on more than their individual motivations and skills. As Michael highlights, BASE is a small community, and word of mouth counts for a great deal. I witnessed this phenomenon firsthand (and was complicit in its reproduction) when a course instructor asked me for my opinion of a skydiver with whom he thought I might be familiar. Though I did not have much to offer, I was nevertheless flattered that, as a neophyte BASE jumper, I would be consulted on such matters. This was a signal that my judgment was taken seriously, that I was (becoming) part of the community. Moreover, I have little doubt that, had I better knowledge of the jumper in question, I would have rendered my opinion, thereby more actively reproducing this kind of boundary maintenance.

BASE ethics

Informal regulation continues to operate for those who have progressed beyond beginner status. This is particularly evident in what is known as BASE ethics. This notion refers to a set of guidelines described in the study materials I received in preparation for my first-jump course. Here, I include the most important of these:

> BASE jumping has it's [*sic*] own peculiar set of ethical guidelines. These ethics have evolved (and continue to do so) over time. The underlying motivation of BASE ethics is our shared desire to jump, and to do so while avoiding arrest or injury. The bottom line aim of BASE ethics is to allow us all to continue making as many jumps as possible in the long run. It follows, then, that actions which make it harder for others to jump are generally viewed as unethical, to some (varying) degree . . .
>
> Contact the Locals: Whether you are a new jumper . . . or a more experienced jumper who is traveling, the original rule of BASE ethics still applies. Always make genuine efforts to locate jumpers local to any object you want to jump from. Not only will this help you meet some wonderful, interesting people, but it will help show respect for the hard work of those who opened (and maintain) site access.

Jumpers let each other choose their own path, but the clear expectation is that one's path does not inhibit the ability of others to follow *their* own paths. As James explained,

> You don't just kind of bring your rig with you and jump off whatever you can see. It's, part of BASE ethics is getting in touch with locals. And that is good for them, and it's also good for you because this beautiful object that you're seeing and thinking, "Hey, I'm going to jump that." Someone might have been busted on there, like two weeks ago, in which case, you know, the object is hot [under police surveillance] and the odds that you're going to get busted there are also very, very good. And so it kind of gives you some more information about the objects. Also for the people who are local, that way, in general you have some idea that stuff that's local to you, is not just being jumped without your knowledge and it gives you a little bit more sense that you know what's going on when you head out to jump something. You're not gonna be suddenly surprised that the police are watching this building that you're hoping to jump.

The seriousness of the expectation to "contact the locals" is highlighted by the case of John Vincent, who, many years ago, traveled to Atlanta and, without contacting the locals, jumped a crane. Previously, a local crew of jumpers had worked out an agreement with the crane operator that he would leave the crane facing in a favorable direction for the jumpers (contrary to company guidelines) in return for a quantity of beer that the jumpers would leave for him each time they jumped it. This arrangement had worked well for locals, as well as jumpers visiting the Atlanta area, until Vincent's "self-aggrandizing video jump" (http://www.BASEjumper.com/Articles/Philosophy/Contact_the_Locals_694.html, retrieved November 26, 2010). Not only did Vincent jump the crane, but he proceeded to publicize the jump. As a result of the ensuing press coverage, the crane came under much tighter security, the construction company initiated an investigation, and the crane operator who had been friendly to local jumpers lost his job. In breaking the "contact the locals" rule, then, Vincent upset local BASE jumpers enough that they were willing to drive several hours to punish him. I describe the confrontation that ensued in the following field note from my first-jump course:

> On the final day of the course, we watched several videos. One was a grainy, dated video documenting the vigilante justice doled out by an Atlanta crew after John Vincent burned their crane. They drove several hours, showed up at his door, forced their way inside, and proceeded to literally tar and feather him. As they rolled out plastic sheeting in his living room (to protect his carpet), he started freaking out, clearly confused and overwhelmed by what was going on. (August 2007)

Video footage of this confrontation is somewhat folkloric in the community. Even jumpers who had not seen the video themselves invoked it when talking about BASE ethics: "It's since become a really famous example of, you don't just go and take away someone else's object" (James). The Atlanta crew's extreme displeasure with this turn of events, their chosen form of exacting justice, and the fact that this video is still in (limited) circulation in the BASE community over a decade later speak to the centrality of "BASE ethics" in a sport in which word of mouth is critical.

3.   emotion, risk, and responsibility

in this chapter (a revised and edited version of a recent paper; see Laurendeau 2011), I draw heavily on autoethnography in order to elaborate on ideas presented in Chapters 1 and 2. Most centrally, I argue that in order to understand how serious leisure participants engage in their "careers," we must consider loyalties and commitments they have to other pursuits (e.g., their work; see Anderson 2011), activities (e.g., other forms of leisure), and people (especially family).

As I argue elsewhere (Laurendeau 2008), too much of the work on voluntary risk activities neglects attention to social actors' other identity projects, relationships, and responsibilities. At the very least, this work devotes too little attention to these issues, though some recent contributions go some way towards addressing this problem (see Anderson 2011). Risk sport participants' passions, choices, and emotions must be considered *in relation to* who they understand themselves to be, and who they understand themselves to be to and for others.

may 2007

After he had done a couple of jumps himself, Jeremy, a jumper and friend with whom I've been talking about BASE for years, floors me: "So, how serious are you about wanting to do a jump?"

My stomach jumps into my throat, my fingers tingling. Jeremy's question takes me back to those Decembers of my childhood when I was so impatient to open Christmas gifts that I actually snuck around the house, found as many as I could, then unwrapped them, rewrapped them, and put them back where I found them. "Are you for real?!" I exclaim.

* * *

As my research assistant and I wait for our maki rolls, I fidget with my disposable chopsticks: rub them together to smooth them out, fit them into my hand, tap them lightly on the table top to line them up just right, then do it all over again.

"You seem nervous," my research assistant ventures.

"More like terrified," I reply.

"It'll be ok," she offers.

"I know it'll be ok," I say, chuckling a bit flippantly. "I'm about to jump off a bridge—I'd be worried if I wasn't scared at this point." Then I go back to my chopsticks.

When we meet back up with the guys, Jeremy goes through the pack job with me, wanting to be sure I am comfortable with the gear he is lending me. My stomach is in my throat. After inspecting the gear and approving Jeremy's pack job, I don his rig. Before we step onto the bridge itself, we practice the climbover and exit, over and over; we aren't going anywhere until I get it right. "Keep your head high," Jeremy says 15 times. I concentrate on this and nothing else. My only job on this exit is to leave in good body position.

Finally satisfied with my launch, Jeremy says: "Let's head to the exit." I look like a deer in headlights—of that I have no doubt. We walk to the exit, talk (again) about the wind conditions, the landing area, the obstacles, and the outs (especially the river). Jeremy says, "Don't forget—clothes dry faster than bones heal."

As instructed, I spit over the edge of the bridge, watching my spittle fall away, its drift telling me about wind direction and strength. After struggling to generate enough spit for a second time, I get the same result. Before putting my helmet on, I wipe the sweat from my brow and rub the bridge of my nose methodically, wishing for a drink of water as I do so. We do a final gear check, and Jeremy readies my pilot chute. "Ready when you are."

From that moment on, I don't notice a single car crossing the bridge. There are hundreds, no doubt, but I am not aware of even one. I am so focused on the railing, and on what I have to do, that everything else disappears. My heart is like a jackhammer in my chest. I grip the railing as hard as I can, my heavy breathing deafening me as I do so. I ease one leg up and over, (unnecessarily) pinching the railing between my legs, terrified of what might happen if my grip loosens. Hugging the railing as I roll over, I focus on turning in the right direction: toward, rather than away from, Jeremy. Once I am over the rail, I have both feet back on the bridge, but the space looks so much smaller from this side! I am generally quite comfortable with heights, but it seems as if I will plummet if I move one centimeter in the wrong direction. Mouth parched, I take my time getting a good grip with both hands, shifting first one hand then the other in the tiniest of movements. My legs bounce a little, almost imperceptibly, much as they did at the point of exhaustion when I used to rock climb. As I look down (which I had just been instructed *not* to do), the edges of the canyon compress inward and the bridge shifts slightly in my vision. Looking back up, I make an effort to breathe through my nose. I take a deep breath, look forward, and say "3, 2, 1, see ya." (This makes it sound as if I am as cool as a cucumber, but I am merely repeating what I've heard other BASE jumpers say.)

I bend my knees slightly, anticipating the "point of no return" of which other jumpers have spoken. As I extend my legs and begin to launch, I feel it. Though my weight is moving off of the bridge, the balls of my feet, light as air, are still in contact with the hard concrete. In real time, there is the briefest moment of total peace, and yet it seems to stretch on forever. Calmness. Clarity. There is no more anticipation, no more "what if?"; I am about to answer the "what if?" one way or another. Then the peace is shattered by the onset of freefall. Time goes from being distended to tremendously compressed as I accelerate away from the bridge, my mind going into business mode: *Good launch—chest high. There's the bridle going taut. There's the pin, the container opening, line stretch, and an inflated parachute flying on heading.*

As I recover my sense of time, I have the weirdest thought, as if I am outside of myself watching: *everything's fine, maybe you should celebrate.* I whoop and holler as loud as possible. As I approach the landing area, I revel in the familiar feeling of a parachute responding to toggle input. I turn to face into the wind for landing, flare, and almost *run* past the camera that happens to be there for a media event. Ignoring the camera crew, I breathe deeply, then gather my lines, slowly looking around me at the landing area, the river, the obstacles, and the bridge itself. *This is not going to be a one-shot deal.*

"if you're reading this . . ."

Once I jumped, I couldn't stop thinking about doing it again, about learning to do it on my own. I genuinely love the feeling of being scared by something, facing that fear, and jumping into it. There's a kind of confidence that comes from that, one that translates into other areas of my life (Lyng 1990). There's more though. I'd be lying if I said I don't get off on other people telling me I'm crazy for the stuff I do. I'm the one who will jump out of something, off of something, or just climb the stone fireplace at a ski chalet while a bunch of friends are having an impromptu dance party below, and this has become part of my masculine identity (Olstead 2011). So, a few months after my first jump, I am off to Idaho again to learn not only how to *do* a BASE jump but how to *be* a BASE jumper.

After 14 hours of driving and a fitful night of sleep, I meet Cam at a diner he likes for breakfast. There is the usual small talk while we eat—how the drive was, catching up on jumpers we both know. I wolf down my breakfast and eagerly engage with him, both because I like him and because I can't wait to learn what he has to teach me. Soon, we are down to business—not the business of how to jump, the business of "you had better be sure this is what you want." Cam presents his well-rehearsed spiel:

> Expect to get injured. And seriously injured means a stay in the hospital. You can avoid getting killed, but the only way to be sure is to walk away. You will also become great friends with some very good people, you'll share great experiences with them, and then you will watch them die. You can count on that. And you may very well die yourself.

None of what he is saying is news, and I don't have much of a reaction. Perhaps that should be a red flag. But it isn't. Or maybe I am just prepared to ignore red flags. Or maybe a red flag means multiple things to me; it could be both a warning and an enticement. Cam proceeds to recount various gruesome injuries and deaths in the sport. *I get it, I get it. I could get hurt. I could get killed. Got it. Now, when do we jump?* Next, Cam gets me to write a letter to my family, explaining to them that I have died:

> If you're reading this, it's because i've died doing a base jump. First of all, please understand that this was my choice. Nobody coerced me into participating in this sport. It's hard for me to describe to you why i chose to take these risks, but suffice it to say that jumping made me feel more alive than anything else. It taught me things about myself that i could learn nowhere else. Please understand that i fully understood the risks of the sport and accepted them as part of my participation.
>
>   I'm sorry to be putting you through this ordeal. Honestly, the risk to myself was not the most difficult part for me to make sense of.

The toughest part of this is the knowledge that i might subject you to the kind of ordeal you now face. Know that i love all of you, and will miss you terribly. If i haven't had this conversation with you in person, i deeply apologize for that. I am afraid to do so, but i will do my best to suck it up and talk to you about this. I want to ask you not to blame anyone else for this. This is not the fault of any other jumper, instructor, or anyone else, and it would disappoint me greatly if they were to get dragged into this in any way.

there is little more i can say at this point. I hope that this helps you all, in some small way, to understand what i've done and why i did it, and to make some sense of my death.

Please understand that this is not about how i died, but about how i lived.

I love you all,

Jay (letter written in August 2007)

In this letter, I am saying what I am supposed to say, but I am so taken up with the excitement of jumping that I am not really checked in with Cam or what he is saying. My letter implies that I am willing to die for what I got out of BASE. Nothing could be further from the truth. Though some of the jumpers I interviewed spend a great deal of time thinking of this and have come to the conclusion that the risks are worth it, that is not me. As I write this letter to my family, I still don't think I could die. In skydiving, I thought I'd be safe because I was young, fit, and coordinated. As I embark on my BASE career, I am no longer as young, or as fit, or as coordinated as I once was. As I listen to Cam recount stories of deaths and injuries in BASE, though, I think I am smart enough to make choices that won't put me in that position (see Laurendeau 2006). I even say to Cam during the course that I am glad to be doing this in my 30s; I don't feel a need to prove anything, so I am more measured in my choices. Clearly, though, I'm not listening. "The *only* way to be sure is to walk away." But I don't walk away. At least not yet.

This letter also illustrates a self-absorption that troubles me. Though I point out my difficulty in coming to terms with the effect my death would have on my family, once again I am not checked in. Though I don't think I will die in BASE, I clearly understand this to be a possibility. And yet there's little evidence in the letter that I take my responsibilities to and for loved ones terribly seriously (Laurendeau 2008; Olstead 2011). Cam's practice of having student jumpers write this letter is perhaps illustrative of a "risk culture" (see Donnelly 2004) in which individuals and organizations seek to protect themselves from potential legal problems.

As I worked on an earlier version of this chapter, I shared it with my mother, who said that my " 'letter' really wouldn't have cut it." She pointed out that my death would have hit my grandmother the hardest and would have left everyone with unanswered questions. And yet, my myopia allows me to jump with a relatively clear conscience—for a while, at least.

"the chief"

Having set out well before dawn, Axel (a local jumper) and I arrive at the trailhead in the dark. Yesterday, when the winds had been too high for us to jump, Axel showed me the landing zone, a little construction area separated from the Chief by a busy highway. There are power lines around the area but a nice big open "runway" if you fly a smart landing pattern. All that's left now is to hike to the exit, talk about the launch, and then do it. The Chief is different from my previous jumps. This is a 1,500 foot cliff, but because of the rock formation it is only "300 feet to impact," as Axel put it. It is also the first time object strike feels like a real possibility.

As we hike to the exit, my legs and lungs sear from the physical effort of the steep hike while carrying my gear, and my mind races with excitement and apprehension.

The Stawamus Chief (AKA "The Chief"), near Squamish, British Columbia. (Bigchen/Dreamstime.com)

"You feeling OK?" Axel asks for a third time. "Nervous at all?"

"Three out of ten," I lie, both to myself and to him.

We arrive at the exit, a small precipice overlooking the waters of Howe Sound and the peaks of the Tantalus range beyond. "Once I'm ready, I'll let you know," Axel starts. "You move forward to this spot, right here. DO NOT walk over here without gear on. I hate when guys do that—it freaks me out."

"Not a problem," I say, and mean it.

"When we're ready, line yourself up with that peak," he continues. "Now, when you're open, once you're happy with everything, hang a ninety left right away. You can fly right along this gorgeous cliff face for a good long while. Just make sure to cross the highway above 500 feet so you don't freak drivers out too much."

"Got it," I reply, thinking about the phrase "300 feet to impact."

"How about now?" Axel asks again. "How are you feeling about everything?"

"I'm pretty freakin' scared, actually." There's no point in lying, I figure. First of all, I'm sure it's written all over my face. Second, I am trusting this guy with my life, literally. Why would I be anything but honest with him?

"Glad to hear it," he replies thoughtfully. "The guys I bring up here who aren't scared, or tell me they aren't scared, are the ones I worry about."

I do a final gear check, caressing my container with my fingertips as I do so. I look around the exit area but not beyond the edge of the cliff, and I don my helmet. I feel a bit like Darth Vader, the sound of my breathing pounding in my ears. I measure each step as I move steadily, but slowly, into position in front of Axel, still six feet from the cliff's edge. I feel slight tugs on my container as Axel checks my gear, extracts my pilot chute from its sleeve, and folds it and my bridle in preparation for "short-lining" me.

"Ready," says Axel, and I feel complete trust in this man I met only 24 hours earlier. He doesn't say a word to me as I inch forward, listening to the scratching of pebbles on the cliff as I grind them into the ground. I work myself into position, looking only at the rock in front of me. *There, that's solid. Yup, solid. Now breathe. Look to that peak on the horizon. Breathe.* "3,2,1, see ya."

As I launch my weight over the edge, I catch my breath just like I do on a hike, when I crest a saddle and a whole new valley opens up in front of me. Then the stillness ends, and I'm falling. *Bridle. Pin. Wow—that cliff is close! Line stretch. Canopy inflated and on heading. TURN LEFT!*

I turn, and the granite monolith is 40 feet away, stretching below me forever. I turn slight left, flying closer and closer, until it feels like the edge of my canopy is only a few feet away from the cliff face. I can't take my eyes off of it, wanting to scorch it into my memory forever. I am alone in the world, it seems, in the very best sense.

Suddenly, over my right shoulder, I hear: "How awesome was that?" I turn and glance at Axel, set against the backdrop of Mount Sedgwick, bathed in the early-morning light. Having jumped a few seconds after I did, he is now flying just a few feet away.

"Freaking amazing!" I answer, tasting the inadequacy of the words.

"Keep playing for a while," he says. "But make sure to cross the highway above 500 feet." I listen carefully, both because I want to be safe and because I want Axel's approval. I look around, making sure I still have time to "play." *How many people have had a view like this?* I smile with my whole heart as I live this moment.

Finally, I have no choice but to pull myself away from the wonder of the cliff face. I apply light pressure to my right toggle, greeting my canopy as if it is a familiar friend. By the time I flare and land, Axel has landed, taken his helmet off, and is holding his camera in his hands, filming my landing.

I am oblivious to Axel and his camera, though, as I turn to look up at the Chief. I stand, slack-jawed, rubbing my closely shorn, balding head, taking in the preceding five minutes. My reverie is interrupted by the sound of gravel under tires, giving away the approach of a pickup truck carrying two well-tanned and muscled construction workers.

"Did you guys just jump off that freaking cliff?!" the passenger asks as the truck rolls to a stop. My lips part slightly, and an un-self-conscious smile takes possession of my face. "Yup," I reply, looking him in the eye.

He exclaims, "That's freaking awesome!!"

Axel places the camera on the hood of the truck, and the four of us gather around it, watching in silence as the video shows me falling away from the cliff face and Axel following shortly behind. The construction workers' respect, and Axel's approval, are palpable as we huddle together around the tiny screen.

antenna

I encounter my first illegal jump in October 2007. (Actually, as is often the case, it is not the jump that is illegal, but the trespassing involved.) This is also the most demanding jump I've done in the sense that the antenna is only 220 feet high. Though I've heard of experienced jumpers doing objects much lower than this, this is by far my lowest to date. Assuming my parachute opens quickly and on-heading, I will barely have time to turn into the wind for landing. Whereas object strike was my big fear on the cliff, altitude (or lack thereof) is my worry on this night.

We wait for a break in traffic (the antenna is located near a major highway) and shimmy under a little gap in the fence, my heart racing, seduced by breaking the law. I am surprised at how physically taxing it is to climb the antenna. My forearms are screaming by the time we reach the top of the long, cramped ascent up an enclosed ladder. And the sound of my rig rubbing up against the enclosure seems deafening. We are out here at about 2 a.m. (to avoid the police), and I am freezing by the time we reach the top of the ladder and step onto the platform.

As I don my rig and adjust my leg straps, I am somewhat distracted. I glance at the field below and spot one of my best friends, with whom I have always wanted to share this experience. And yet, even with Roger's presence, I do not feel "amped" about this jump. Jeff spends 20 minutes meticulously preparing the equipment on the outer rail, explaining what he's doing as he goes. I don't seem to care. *Let's just do this.* Eventually, we jump into the cold night air, landing in the field below. I whoop and holler, but it is not entirely heartfelt.

my last one

As it turns out, my one and only antenna jump was also my last jump. The last notable turning point in my brief BASE career happened outside of the sport: I met Carly. Carly is not particularly impressed by parachutes or stories of being a bad boy. She is impressed by passion, by vulnerability and honesty, and by people who love with abandon. And she is and does these things in spades.

Though my decision to leave BASE was cemented the day our son was born, it was a work in progress for the preceding 16 months. BASE—or any serious leisure pursuit (Stebbins 2007)—demands an enormous commitment of time and energy. With Carly and I forming a new relationship and each of us negotiating the early stages of an academic career, BASE got shelved. And as was always the case with skydiving, the longer I went between jumps, the easier it was to ignore the itch to do another one. Carly and I rarely talked about BASE. It was something she didn't necessarily understand or appreciate, but she knew that it was a path I had chosen and that I had to work through its place in *my* life as we forged *our* new life together. Not that this "working through" happened actively, though. In fairly short order, the rewards I received from my participation in BASE seemed less important to me, less tangible. The intensity of emotion associated with a jump fades as the jump itself recedes into memory. The anticipation of another jump prolongs that process, but only for so long. The rewards of my relationship with Carly, on the other hand, were and are patently obvious.

At the same time, the risks of BASE suddenly had more weight to them, especially when Carly and I started talking about having a baby (see Laurendeau 2008). The vast majority of jumpers I spoke to said they would have to think very seriously about whether or not to keep jumping if and when they have children. For me and for other jumpers I spoke to, this is not a simple equation where a small child equals quitting BASE. I met a number of jumpers who continued jumping with children. It becomes one important part, though, of how you make sense (or don't) of your participation. And in my case, it became *the* important part.

dear quinn

I find myself wondering, from time to time, if I would have stayed with BASE had I been doing it longer before Carly and I met, and before Quinn came along. At the end of the day, though, I hadn't. And at that point in my nascent BASE jumping career, there wasn't enough tying me to the sport. I took every opportunity to do a jump over the course of those few months after my first one, but my commitment hadn't been cemented by the time things shifted dramatically. The "durable benefits" (Stebbins 2007) of BASE all but vaporized when I met Carly, and even more so when Quinn was born. I still get excited (really excited!) by watching a BASE film at the Banff Mountain Film Festival, for example. But the durable benefits in my life are to be found principally (though not exclusively) in my relationships with Carly and Quinn. I may never again experience the particular kind of emotionality that came with parachuting from a cliff. But that is not something that I carry around with me. What I carry around with me, what "puts me together," is the sense of awe that accompanies my journey towards understanding myself as a man, a partner, and a father:

Dear Quinn:
  One of the first times I met your mom, I was packing a parachute on my front lawn. I'm sure she thought I was nuts, but to me, it made all

the sense in the world that I would be willing to jump from a bridge or a cliff. Until recently, those were the most intense emotional experiences I'd ever had. Not only were they exhilarating, but they helped me find a part of myself that I couldn't find anywhere else.

I still get excited by the thought of doing a BASE jump. There was a time when I thought the potential price to be paid was worth it. You and your mom helped me understand that I'm no longer willing to take that chance. True, I could die doing just about anything, but the hazards were greater in BASE jumping. And that's not a price I'm willing to pay at this stage of my life (and our lives together). After a number of years where I felt like I was searching for something, I am now thoroughly enjoying having found it, and that has everything to do with you and your mom.

Quinn, let me tell you about the minutes after you were born. While the doctors and nurses worked to check that you and your mom were all right, I basically stood there and cried. It was the happiest moment of my life. I'm not a religious guy, but there was something much bigger than me in the hospital room that day. There's a great picture from that day of me looking at your mom, with my hand on her left cheek, my head turned a bit, a look of total awe on my face. I've seen a look kind of like that on my face one other time as I stared up at a mountain, but this one, my love, is the one that will stay with me forever.

You were the most amazing thing I'd ever seen. I stood there with my hand on your tiny chest and just felt you breathe, and bawled my eyes out. I could see right through your ribs, could almost watch the blood flowing through your veins as you were introduced to what must have seemed like such a harsh world. And I knew right then that it was our job to keep you safe. That moment is a huge part of why I sold my BASE gear last summer. I thought I'd feel sad doing that, but I really didn't. It felt like I was selling something from a different lifetime.

I thought that BASE taught me some things about myself, and it did. I've learned far more in the last few years from the hours your mom and I spent talking about our lives, what we wanted from ourselves and from each other. We talked about this stuff as we hiked together, traveled together, worked together, you name it. I've also learned them from watching you as you negotiate the world and figure out how your body works, who you can trust, and that we will always be there to celebrate your successes and help you up when things don't go according to plan. And I couldn't have learned those things by jumping from a bridge.

I love you, beautiful boy . . .

Dad (letter first composed in October 2009)

4. origins and developments

though I have endeavored to capture the history of BASE jumping as accurately and comprehensively as possible, this is a daunting task. The principal reason for this is that there exist multiple histories of the activity (and of the history of parachuting more generally), even among practitioners who take the roots of the activity seriously. Chris McDougall, one of the most skilled jumpers in BASE, recently wrote a book about his experiences in the activity and included a discussion of its history. As he noted in an email, "The history is interesting, people think its all american [*sic*] but it totally isn't, I even [messed] a bit of it up in my book." I also spoke with one jumper who was intimately involved in the very early years of BASE's modern history, who went one step further. This person suggested that "old-timers" are likely to give you one version of the sport's history, while you would get quite a different version from jumpers who have come onto the scene more recently. What is sociologically interesting, assuming that this assertion has merit, is how and why the history of BASE has been revised to this extent. In any case, this makes the task of constructing a history of BASE both exciting and daunting. Jeb Corliss, an icon in BASE, added two additional layers to the challenge of writing a history of the activity. First, he suggested that we have little evidence of the very earliest examples of people jumping from fixed objects (over a thousand years ago now). There are occasional written accounts that have been translated, and so we can draw some conclusions but perhaps with a degree of caution. More importantly, he suggests that there are "hidden histories" that will never be captured in the record. Corliss has little doubt that hundreds—or even thousands—of years ago, someone, or even several people, took up the idea of jumping from a fixed object, and these efforts were never documented in any way. As Corliss points out, we will never be able to capture these as part of the history of the sport. Additionally, this means that the early history, especially, is replete with examples of people "reinventing the wheel" because the phenomenon of sharing information widely with fellow practitioners is, historically speaking, an extremely recent development.

As I consider various events and developments over more than a millennium, I highlight the dominant version of the history of BASE. As I do so, however, I outline evidence that troubles this history. In addition, I draw on archival research to offer a detailed account of one relatively brief period in the history of BASE—the late 1970s to the early 1980s. I focus on this period for two main reasons. First, this era is often thought of as the time of the birth of the modern activity. A detailed consideration of the events in this era will allow me to both elaborate on and complicate this received version of events. Second, as a case study, this research permits a consideration of both efforts to regulate the activity and the development of BASE as an activity separate from skydiving (as opposed to a subdiscipline thereof). I conclude by considering some of the most important developments of the last three decades.

early dreams of flight

While BASE jumping, as a form of recreation, is in its infancy, the idea of jumping from fixed objects and landing safely is now over a millennium old. In order to understand the contemporary sport of BASE, we must first consider early dreams of flight and the individuals who endeavored to bring those dreams to life. The history of the parachute is often traced to the ideas of Leonardo da Vinci and the sketches of Fausto Veranzio produced in 1595. Evidence is somewhat sporadic and contradictory, but a number of observers suggest that the concept of a parachute can be traced even further, to twelfth-century China. Archival evidence seems to indicate the use of parachute-like devices as part of stunt displays performed to entertain guests of the Chinese courts. Even earlier, however, we find the occasional reference to an inventor devising a contraption with the aim of "flying" from a tall building. Lienhard (2006) suggests that in the ninth century CE, Abbas Ibn Firnas (sometimes spelled ibn-Firnas), a "young Berber astronomer and poet from North Africa [became] one of the earliest named and documented humans who really flew" (21–22). After witnessing a daredevil jump in 852 in which the jumper descended from a tower using a "wing-like cloak," Ibn Firnas set to work creating a glider built to carry a human. In 875, he jumped from a tower as well, and the device proved to be a success though Ibn Firnas sustained a back injury due to a bad landing. The jump is described by Rough (2006/2007, 29–30):

> . . . with a horde watching in Moorish Spain, the respected physician Abbas ibn-Firnas covered his body with Buzzard feathers, climbed a high wall, and raised a pair of wings. Though he is said to have glided some distance, he smashed to the ground and broke his back. Chronicling ibn-Firnas' attempt, a sympathetic critic wrote that "not knowing that birds when they alight come down upon their tails, he forgot to provide himself with one."

Over the next few centuries, we see other examples of inventors and adventurers of various descriptions devising their own designs for contraptions that (they believed) would allow them to leap from tall structures and descend safely to earth. For example, in the early eleventh century, Eilmer of Malmesbury, a Benedictine monk, "outfitted himself with feathered wings, both for his arms and feet, and [jumped from] the top of Malmesbury Abbey" (Rough 2006/2007, 30; see also White 1978). This jump was one of the most successful of these early attempts in that Eilmer is said to have covered over 600 feet before landing. White (1978, 59), in fact, argues that Eilmer is the "first Occidental who can be shown to have flown." The jump was also disastrous, though, because eventually "a combination of wind and panic sent him hurtling to the ground. He broke both legs and remained crippled for the rest of his life" (Rough 2006/2007, 30). Some consider Eilmer to be the earliest aviator, in part because of the strength of the evidence of his "flight." He is said to have claimed that his disastrous landing was the result of his failure to include a tail in his design (Rough 2006/2007).

Though dreams of flight can be traced back well over a millennium, the earliest drawings of a parachute resembling modern designs are often attributed to Leonardo da Vinci. In 1483, he sketched a parachute design in his notebook with the following note: "If a man is provided with a length of gummed linen cloth with a length of 12 yards on each side and 12 yards high, he can jump from any great height whatsoever without injury." Da Vinci himself, though, never tested his design. In fact, it would be over 500 years before anyone would do so.

On June 25, 2000, British adventurer Adrian Nicholas finally tested da Vinci's parachute. Nicholas, then 38 years of age, was an extremely experienced skydiver, having logged roughly 6,500 jumps by that point. His girlfriend Katarina Ollikainen constructed the device, drawing on the expertise of Professor Martin Kemp from Oxford University (some reports suggest that Ollikainen and Nicholas built the device together). Using only materials that would have been available in the fifteenth century (with the exception of some thick balloon tape to protect the canvas from tearing), Ollikainen constructed the 187-pound device. After two aborted attempts, Nicholas finally jumped 10,000 feet above Mpumalanga Province of South Africa. He descended for 7,000 feet before releasing the contraption and deploying a modern-day parachute, which he landed without incident. Despite the warnings of skeptics (including aeronautics experts), da Vinci's design performed admirably, providing a slow, smooth descent. The only element of da Vinci's design that was not tested by Nicholas's jump was the landing. Even this question was answered in 2008 when Swiss adventurer Olivier Vietti-Teppa jumped a slightly modified version of the design. Having jumped from a helicopter hovering 2,000 feet above the ground, Vietti-Teppa landed, albeit somewhat roughly. In fact, despite Nicholas' equipment being more true to da Vinci's specifications, numerous news outlets heralded Vietti-Teppa's jump as evidence that da Vinci's parachute "worked."

Though Nicholas is most famous for testing Leonardo da Vinci's design for the parachute, this is by no means his only notable achievement. He is also renowned for having undertaken the longest freefall in skydiving history. Nicholas had been on the front lines of the development of wingsuit technology (discussed in greater detail below) and had witnessed the death of his friend and skydiving pioneer Patrick de Gayardon in 1998 as the latter worked on the wingsuit. Nicholas was determined to take up de Gayardon's work. On March 12, 1999, he performed a wingsuit jump from 35,850 feet in an attempt to break the records for longest freefall and most distance covered. "As I stepped out of the aeroplane, the exhaust valve in my oxygen mask froze solid," he later recalled (http://www.telegraph.co.uk/news/obituaries/1498884/Adrian-Nicholas.html, accessed March 21, 2012). Due to the freezing temperatures at this altitude, he could not exhale. Nor could he remove the mask, as he would have died from a lack of oxygen. Eventually, he was able to break the seal slightly, though he remained oxygen deprived for approximately four minutes. Despite these challenges, he remained in freefall for almost five minutes, covering 10 horizontal miles in the process (both records). Sadly, Nicholas died in 2008. As he came in for a high-speed (but routine) landing at a drop zone in Holland, his automatic activation device (AAD) fired, deploying his reserve parachute about 300 feet off the ground. (Having both a "main" and a "reserve" out at the same time can be extremely hazardous, as I describe in greater detail in the next chapter.) Nicholas cut away his main in an effort to land safely, but there was simply not enough remaining altitude for a safe landing under the circumstances. He hit the ground at a high speed and died of his injuries at the scene.

Despite the common association of da Vinci's name with the invention of the parachute, White (1978) argues that this credit rightly belongs to an unnamed Italian engineer. Drawing on archival research, White suggests that a number of drawings—some of them outlining conical parachute designs similar to that produced by da Vinci—appear in an Italian manuscript that dates from 1470 at the latest. White contends that da Vinci did not come to his "invention" independently but rather developed and refined the design of this Italian engineer:

> It is indicative of Leonardo's perceptiveness that he picked up this new idea so quickly and that he began to make it more sophisticated. The scale of his parachute is more realistic for the weight of a man. He replaces the hoop-like wooden base . . . with a simpler base composed of four rods, and this alters the shape of the textile portion from conical to pyramidal. (White 1978, 465)

Just over a century after da Vinci's design, Fausto Veranzio (also known as Faust Vrančić, Verancsics Faustus, or Faust Verantius, depending on the era and language of the source) created a number of illustrations that proved influential in the development of parachute technology. Like da Vinci, Veranzio was interested in mechanics and engineering broadly speaking; he was especially interested in mills, producing insights about windmill designs that remain influential to this day. In *Machinae Novae* (published in 1595 or 1615—there are conflicting reports), Veranzio sketched "Homo Volans" ("The Flying Man"), based, in part at least, on examinations of da Vinci's work. Veranzio is considered by some to be the first to design, build, and test a parachute. In 1617, when Veranzio was well into his 60s, he jumped from St. Mark's Campanile in Venice, Italy. It should be noted that some sources report this jump as taking place in 1595, while others suggest that there is no strong evidence that the jump ever took place. The 1617 jump is mentioned in a 1648 book authored by John Wilkins of the Royal Society in London.

Homo volans, Fausto Veranzio, 1615. (Library of Congress)

It would be the early twentieth century before the modern parachute, based to a certain extent on da Vinci's and Veranzio's designs, would see any meaningful acceptance. In the intervening centuries, inventors and adventurers continued their efforts to construct flying apparatuses of different designs. As just one example of these continued efforts, a locksmith by the name of Jacob Besnier tested one such device in the late seventeenth century in the French town of Sablé. Besnier's design consisted of two poles with flappers. Using both hands and feet, the wearer could generate a flapping motion. This, in principal, would allow "a man to fly some distance from a height—perhaps down the street, or over a small river. Besnier tried his device from a stool, then from a table, then from a window. Finally, he leapt from a high garret" (Rough 2006/2007, 39). Besnier is said not to have "flown" far, if at all, and spent some time healing broken bones after his attempt.

Again, historians disagree on the strength of the evidence for various "firsts" outlined in this chapter. White (1978, 179), for example, suggests that there is "no firm evidence that any European actually jumped in any form of parachute until . . . 1783." Louis-Sébastien Lenormand of Montpellier, inspired by tales of acrobats entertaining a seventeenth-century Siamese king, constructed his own design:

> On December 26, equipped with two umbrellas re-enforced by cords running from the tips of the ribs to the bottom of the handles, Lenormand climbed an elm in a private garden and successfully leaped from a branch. Public demonstrations ensued, one of which was witnessed by Joseph Montgolfier, and Lenormand coined the word "parachute." (White 1978, 466)

The late eighteenth century proved to be a period of feverish activity with respect to parachuting. André-Jacques Garnerin, an important figure in the early history of ballooning, jumped a silk parachute on October 22, 1797, at Parc Monceau, Paris. The parachute resembled a closed umbrella, with a center pole and a rope running through the pole, which connected the contraption to Garnerin's balloon. Garnerin later said:

> I was on the point of cutting the cord that suspended me between heaven and earth . . . and measured with my eye the vast space that separated me from the rest of the human race. . . . I felt myself precipitated with a velocity which was checked by a sudden unfolding

of my parachute. . . . At length I perceived thousands of people, some
on horseback, others on foot, following me, all of whom encouraged
me by their wishes, while they opened their arms to receive me.
(Quoted in Soden 2005, 19)

Garenerin's attempt was initially met with much skepticism, arising in
part from past failed or aborted efforts. Even his assistant reportedly experienced trepidation, later writing "I made all my efforts to dissuade him to
try this perilous enterprise" (quoted in Soden 2005, 21).

Jeanne-Geneviève, Garnerin's wife, would later become the first
woman parachutist and a regular participant in parachuting demonstra-
tions alongside her husband. Her story, though, illustrates an important
pattern in both popular and academic historical research, one that is certainly evident in histories of parachuting and BASE jumping. All too
often, historians gloss over, or neglect altogether, the contributions of
women in histories of adventure activities. Unfortunately, the result is that
the importance of these women is often rather underexplored, to say the
least. While it is possible, for example, to find numerous detailed sources
about the career of André-Jacques Garnerin, little is said about Jeanne-
Geneviève in the vast majority of these sources. We will see the same pattern in evidence with respect to important pioneers in early (modern)
BASE jumping, especially Jean Boenish. From most documents, it seems
that her contribution was mainly as the wife of Carl Boenish, often considered the "father" of BASE. Too little is said about her unique contributions to the activity, both while her husband was alive and in the years
and decades that followed. As sport historian Carly Adams notes, "silen-
ces in historical scholarship do not mean absences" (Adams 2008, 1).
While I endeavor to address this shortcoming in this volume, I am limited
by available information. Much more work is needed in bringing to light
the contributions of these women who were important in their own right.

The importance of André-Jacques and Jeanne-Geneviève Garnerin not-
withstanding, early balloonists were generally skeptical about the use of
the parachute. This was because of both the unnecessary weight and the
social implications of its use as a safety device. At a time when balloonists
were interested in captivating public interest and making money, carrying a
parachute raised questions about the courage of the pilot and implied a lack
of confidence in the technology of the balloon itself as a flying device. In
1838, for example, American balloonist John Wise exploded his balloon
at 13,000 feet and safely descended using fragments of the bag. This, he

argued, was evidence that a damaged balloon was more valuable than a parachute. The parachute gained legitimacy first through its use by carnival stunt performers and later by military personnel. Stunt parachutists, both men and women, were popular carnival acts in both Europe and North America through the nineteenth century. Risk-taking and "cheating death" were constructed as popular media and spectator events that included the daring tightrope walkers and barrel plunges over Niagara Falls.

The first modern recorded descents from fixed objects occurred near the turn of the twentieth century. In 1879, for example, H. P. Peer performed the first of a number of jumps from the Upper Suspension Bridge near Niagara Falls, Canada. Another well-known (and documented) jump from this era was Frederick Law's 1912 jump from the Statue of Liberty. Little is known about Law, and it seems he wanted it that way. Yet Law's jump from the Statue of Liberty is a perfect exemplar of the kinds of jumps undertaken in what we might call the early-modern history of BASE jumping. These early jumps were stunts in the sense that they were performed by a handful of people, many of them accomplished performers, who generally did one or two such jumps in a lifetime. Law's jump was described in a *New York Times* article from February 3, 1912. I quote this article at some length here because it is the earliest popular-press article describing a fixed-object jump (it would not be called BASE until the early 1980s) and perhaps the only one of its kind in a publication with the circulation and prestige of the *New York Times*:

> Frederick R. Law . . . decided yesterday to startle the world with an entirely original feat. . . . According to one of his foremen, the boss steeplejack sat in his office all yesterday morning looking over the city's high towers. . . . [Eventually,] the happy alternative of the Statue of Liberty suggested itself, and at noon the aerial contractor set out for Bedlow's Island.

By 2:00 p.m., Law had secured a special permit to jump, and soon a large crowd of spectators, including some with "moving picture machines," began to assemble. Law jumped at 2:45 p.m.:

> . . . There was fear of a tragedy for a moment, for the steeplejack fell fully seventy-five feet like a dead weight, the parachute showing no inclination whatever to open at first.
>
> When it opened the wind blew it clear of the statue. Then Law began waving his hands frantically. It was not a sign of alarm, merely

Evidence suggests that the first "stunt" at Niagara Falls (as opposed to the Niagara River rapids) was undertaken by Anna Taylor on October 24, 1901: "Assistants strapped her . . . into a special harness in a barrel. A small boat towed the barrel out into the main stream of the Niagara River and the barrel was cast loose" (see http://www.niagaraparks.com/media/niagara-falls -stunting-history.html, accessed December 29, 2011). (Library of Congress)

a steering method which the young aeronaut had adopted to keep his craft out of the bay. It proved practical, too, for the parachute descended gracefully.

Not all of these early jumps were stunts, strictly speaking. In some cases, jumpers continued the line of serious inventors and parachute pioneers. Franz Reichelt, sometimes referred to as the "Flying Tailor," is a case in point. In 1912, in his spare time, Reichelt worked on what Rough (2006/2007, 33) describes as a "voluminous black overcoat." Reichelt included wooden stays in his design as well. The idea was that as the wearer jumped, the coat would open, wings would fill with rushing air, and the coat would enable the jumper to descend safely. Rough (2006/2007) speculates that in light of the number of people who have jumped or fallen from the Eiffel Tower, Reichelt's jump from this structure might have been lost to history had it not been filmed. Rough describes what can be seen in the footage (and his interpretation thereof):

> In the first skipping frames of mote-flecked black-and-white, Reichelt modeled the overcoat. . . . Reichelt had experimented with the overcoat from a height of ten or twelve feet. It is not clear what happened; perhaps, after leaping from a creek bridge or a rock wall, he blamed his hard landing on the fact that the coat needed more time to completely unfurl. Or maybe, forgetting that it would be quite possible for a human to survive a ten- or twelve-foot drop unaided, he wrongly attributed his survival to the coat. Reichelt received permission to test his suit from the Eiffel Tower. His request said that he planned to make a "dummy drop"—certainly no live person would come down. On a cold February day, scores of onlookers, mostly men, reporters, police, and officials gathered beneath the tower. Imagine their excitement when Reichelt, having just modeled his suit for the camera, decided that he himself should test it. (Rough 2006/2007, 33–34)

Reichelt's decision to test the design himself would cost him his life. It may also explain why, almost a century later, historians continue to discuss his jump. Rough describes Reichelt's ascent to the exit point:

> His figure, black and hulking, crept up 347 steps to the first level of the Eiffel Tower. This is the level just above the arches, 189 feet above the ground. . . . "See you soon," he called to the men around him, cheerily enough . . . (2006/2007, 34–35)

Rough (2006/2007) then describes a 40-second section of the film in which Reichelt hesitates a number of times. Rough suggests that in those seconds, Reichelt may have come to the conclusion that he was about to die but could see no way out of his predicament. Whatever Reichelt's state of mind, though, he eventually launched:

> The foot still planted on the chair came forward, and, with his knees folding in defeat, Reichelt merely crumpled over the rail. The magnificent black over coat wadded and sloughed over the edge. A camera on the ground recorded Reichelt's five-second plummet. (Rough 2006/2007, 35)

airplanes, militarized masculinity, and sport parachuting

The invention of the airplane presented new technical challenges for parachutists, as previous parachute designs relied on the slow movement of balloons, or no movement at all in the case of fixed-object jumps. Further, when freefall was introduced, parachutists had to deal with what would now be called "forward throw." For the first few seconds of falling from a fast-moving aircraft, jumpers would maintain at least some of the forward speed of the aircraft. This changed the behavior of a parachute as it deployed, and became a practical hurdle to overcome.

In addition to the practical issues raised by airplanes, social norms presented hurdles to the acceptance of the parachute. Pilots vowed to stay with their planes, attempting to salvage them until they crashed. The parachute represented a direct affront to the expertise and courage of pilots. However, as the performance of parachutes improved and the possibility of deploying troops as part of military strategy was raised in the era of World War I, a general faith in parachuting began to emerge. Slovac inventor Štefan Banič constructed a prototype parachute and tested it for the United States military, first jumping from a 41-story building in 1913, then from an airplane in 1914. The United States government considers Banič a notable American of Slovac descent. In fact, his name makes an appearance in H.RES.918, which recognized "the contributions of all Slovak-Americans." Banič is mentioned as the inventor of the parachute, appearing alongside such names as Tom Ridge, Andy Warhol, and Paul Newman (http://thomas.loc.gov/cgi-bin/query/z?c111:HRES918:).

The Russians experimented in the 1930s, but it was not until the German paratrooper assault on the island of Crete in 1941 that the military importance of parachuting was recognized. Air forces were interested in parachuting, but the equipment was generally not available; manufacturers could not catch up to military demands until 1942. Institutionalized resistance had given way to a technical optimism through which traditional masculine values could be invoked, particularly when military advantage was at stake.

The emergence of sport parachuting has been attributed to the military influences described above, with particular credit given to the establishment of the British Airborne Forces in 1940. It was not merely the use of military surplus gear by civilian skydivers, however, or the financial and human resources mobilized to improve the technical performance of the parachute that provided the impetus for the sport. Indeed the ideologies linking wartime courage and masculinity had a profound residual impact on sport parachuting. Paratrooping involved the use of one's body in unfamiliar and sometimes terrifying ways. But, obviously, it was in the interests of the military to shape the identities of young men to make sense out of the sacrifice of bodies during war. Instilling a distinct sense of masculinity based on courage, risk, and adventure, fueled by patriotism, was vital to these invocations. Boys were to return home men. For paratrooping, an unbridled faith in technology and the legitimacy of the exercise had to be taken for granted if the following missions on the ground were to be accomplished. And, in a broader context, wars have been utilized to demonstrate new technologies to the extent that they have been legitimized under any pretense of success.

Both the United States and Soviet Union experimented widely with the performance boundaries of the parachute during the 1950s and 1960s. In 1959, as part of Project Excelsior, Colonel (then Captain) Joe Kittinger stepped out of a balloon at 76,400 feet to test high-altitude survival equipment. On August 16, 1960, he jumped from 102,800 feet, establishing a record for the highest successful parachute jump in history (Robinson and Patrick 2008). Though there are discrepancies in the estimates of the maximum speed achieved by Kittinger in freefall (with some suggesting that he broke the sound barrier), researchers have recently modeled the jump and suggested that the more conservative estimate of just over 600 mph is more accurate (Robinson and Patrick 2008). (Interestingly, the higher estimates that these authors reject are often attributed to U.S. military sources.) Massive spending on the advancement of technology

Then-Captain Joe Kittinger undertakes the highest successful parachute jump in history, exiting at 102,800 feet (31,300 m). (U.S. Air Force)

under the backdrop of the Cold War provided the impetus for record breaking and competition. Supposedly there were no boundaries to what could be achieved, and there was little mention of the costs.

The costs mentioned above were not limited to the military, nor were they only financial in nature. As with any risk sport, those who are really pushing the limits, inventing (or reinventing) technologies and techniques, confront extreme hazards as they do so. This is seen in the earliest jumps described above. In addition, it is evident in cases like that of sport jumper Nick Piantanida. In his third attempt to break Kittinger's altitude record (as part of what he called Project Strato-Jump), Piantanida died in 1966 after his equipment malfunctioned. Planning to jump from 120,000 feet, Piantanida suffered brain damage when his oxygen mask depressurized on the ascent. He slipped into a coma from which he never recovered.

The allure of this kind of record was by no means limited to the cold war era. Much more recently, project "Red Bull Stratos" has been organized to "advance scientific discoveries in aerospace for the benefit of mankind [sic]" (http://www.redbullstratos.com/the-mission/what-is-the-mission/, accessed March 24, 2012). The aim is for Felix Baumgartner to conduct a jump from 120,000 feet, and Joe Kittinger serves as an advisor to the project. On March 16, 2012, Baumgartner did a test jump from 71,581 feet, a jump that organizers considered a successful test on the way to the record attempt (http://www.msnbc.msn.com/id/46751279/ns/technology_and _science-space/t/skydiver-passes-halfway-point-quest-make-highest-jump/ #.T23DqHmuGSo, accessed March 24, 2012).

Nick Piantanida, a New Jersey truck driver, attempted to break the record for the world's longest freefall in what he called "Project Strato-Cloud." (Time & Life Pictures/Getty Images)

The residual military meanings of parachuting—self-reliance, team-work, competition, and risk-identity—had a direct impact on sport para-chuting. Militarized forms of masculinity were embedded in the value structures that have been institutionalized within the sport. But main-stream cultural status was not ascribed to skydiving, at least not in its early years. Airport officials were resistant to the shift in parachuting from life-saving exercises and airshow exhibitions to leisure activities in the 1950s. This of course provided more notoriety to civilian parachuting enthusiasts. But by 1963 the Federal Aviation Administration of the United States had established rules and requirements for the sport, with similar regulations developing in other countries (e.g., Laurendeau and Gibbs Van Brunschot 2006). What emerged was a distinct alternative sport culture with its own sets of rituals, awards, standards of proficiency, and even a unique sport parachuting language.

Change in sport parachuting has been based on preserving continuity while sustaining and reproducing notions of progress and challenge. For example, "relative work," or freefalling in close proximity, developed in the late 1950s, leading to larger formations—from a 50-person formation in the late 1970s to a 400-person formation in February 2006. Each gener-ation of parachutists has had the capacity to determine the form and mean-ing of the sport.

Change has also come on the heels of technological improvements such as the introduction of "ram-air" canopy technology, a topic I develop in greater detail in Chapter 5. High-performance elliptical canopies capable of previously unimaginable ground speed and responsiveness are now commonplace (Laurendeau 2006). Yet this is not to suggest that the notion of progress remains uncontested within the skydiving community; some participants, in fact, question the suitability of high-performance canopies and the motivation of those compelled to push the envelope of perfor-mance at greater risk to their well-being and the safety of others (Laurendeau and Gibbs Van Brunschot 2006). It should be noted, how-ever, that the particular technologies that developed in skydiving and BASE respectively were somewhat different, as it became apparent that there were different needs in each activity.

"the cap had never been jumped"

At this point in the history of BASE, we come to what many call the modern era. Iconic jumps from El Capitan, in California's Yosemite

> El Capitan, extending approximately 900 m from base to summit, is a granite monolith that has figured prominently in the history of rock climbing as well. This is explored in some depth in Joseph E. Taylor III's *Pilgrims of the Vertical* (2010).

National Park (YNP), are considered by many to signal the birth of BASE as a recreational activity. However, other jumpers thousands of miles away were engaged in similar activities around the same time and even earlier. Nevertheless, the dominant narrative of the birth of BASE is a touchstone and thus merits a detailed consideration here.

In early 1966, Michael Pelkey and Brian Schubert met at a skydiving drop zone in California. Before long, the two 26-year-olds were talking seriously about the possibility of jumping El Capitan. The motivation, in Pelkey's words, was simple: "The Cap had never been jumped. . . . Our mission was quite simple. We wanted to be the first parachutists to conquer the Cap" (http://www.basejumper.com/Articles/Stories/Mike _Pelkey_El_Capitan_BASE_jump_1966_771.html, accessed March 21, 2012). As he noted elsewhere, "It was more of a lark than a compulsion. Skydiving was a relatively new sport and the El Capitan was obviously jumpable, straight down 3,200 feet off the valley floor. If we hadn't got to it first, someone else inevitably would have" (http://www.articlesbase .com/extreme-sports-articles/an-inspirational-first-base-jump-1249728 .html, accessed March 21, 2012).

Pelkey and Schubert are said to have sowed the seeds for the modern sport of BASE, though this was never their aim. Because of the nature of their equipment (especially round parachutes) and the fact that BASE jumping as a recreational activity was still over a decade away, Pelkey and Schubert had little choice but to "play it by ear." In addition, their research helped them to understand some of the basic features of El Capitan, but, as Pelkey notes, some important information was missing:

We got a few books from the library and studied what we could from them. The only real useful information we could glean was that the El Capitan was a sheer vertical monolith that rose 3,200 feet above the valley floor. Other rather important details such as wind patterns, landing areas, etc., had to be experienced empirically. (http://www .articlesbase.com/extreme-sports-articles/an-inspirational-first-base -jump-1249728.html, accessed March 21, 2012)

As to the possibility of being hurt, Pelkey notes that the two jumpers were "26 years old at the time and thus invincible. Injury or death were the furthest things from our minds. Our only plan involved a celebratory bottle of champagne when we got back to our cabins" (http://www .basejumper.com/Articles/Interviews_and_Profiles/Someone_You_Should _Know . . . 15_Questions_with . . . _Michael_Pelkey_868.html, accessed March 21, 2012). As it turns out, the combination of somewhat unpredictable winds and the limitations of the equipment they were using conspired against the two men and resulted in injuries to both jumpers. Pelkey had difficulty maneuvering his round parachute and suffered an ankle injury when he struck the face of the cliff under canopy. Schubert was injured more severely when his parachute collapsed approximately 50 feet off the ground. Pelkey was skydiving—wearing a small cast— within a month. Schubert, on the other hand, spent some time in the hospital and walked with a limp for the remainder of his life.

The focus on Pelkey and Schubert's jump (and on Carl Boenish's jumps in the late 1970s) seems to reflect something of a North American bias in histories of the sport (certainly in English-language histories). This is not to take away from the accomplishments of these early pioneers, whose contributions and biographies are detailed in this chapter. Rather, it is to suggest that it was not only in the United States that sport parachutists were undertaking the project of jumping from fixed objects (especially cliffs, in the early stages). In the year prior to Pelkey and Schubert's jump, Austrians Erich Felbermayr and Wolfgang Weitzenböck worked out the logistics of jumping a peak in the Italian Dolomites. And in fact there is much better documentation of a 1966 jump by Weitzenböck from Sextener Rotwand in the Sexten Dolomite range in South Tyrol, Italy, than there ever was of Pelkey and Schubert's 1966 jump. The footage appears in *Sensation Alpen*, a West German mountaineering documentary directed by Lothar Brandler. The film was released on December 23, 1966, and includes wonderful footage of Weitzenböck throwing wind drifts, then launching himself from Rotwand and landing safely on the scree slope below. Despite this footage, little has been written (in English, at least) about these jumps or other early European jumps.

Neither Pelkey nor Shubert would undertake another BASE jump for several decades. Nevertheless, they were honored at the 2005 Bridge Day event in West Virginia, where Pelkey also made his second jump. It was around this time that they came to understand the influence that their jump had had on Carl Boenish and other pioneers of the sport of BASE jumping.

At Bridge Day 2006, Schubert made his first jump in 40 years and, sadly, died in the attempt. Matthew happened to be undertaking his first BASE jump at this particular Bridge Day and described the scene in his interview:

> Brian Schubert stepped up to the edge . . . So, had a great view, 'course the announcer, the MC, uh, talked it up. There was a P.A. system. He uh, told the history all about it, and "let's all give a hand for him, it's his first jump back. Let's go." This is something that he wanted to do so we were all cheering and giving him heads up. He gave us a big wave. He stepped up to the edge. He counted and jumped . . . And he slowly rotated onto his back . . . at that point he'd gone down beyond the edge that I could see. He was going low. . . . He continued his rotation until he was belly [to earth]. The pilot chute came out of his hand, whether he threw it or the air let it go. . . . Then he hit the water and that was it. The moment it happened, the whole bridge just went silent. There was never a doubt what had just happened to him.

The scene described by Matthew captures both the stakes of BASE and also the respect and reverence accorded these pioneering jumpers.

modern BASE jumping

What is often referred to as the modern history of BASE jumping was born on August 18, 1978, when Kent Lane leaped from the edge of El Capitan at approximately 9 a.m. He was part of a group of six jumpers, four of whom jumped that day after weeks of preparation. The remaining two—Carl Boenish and Dave Blattel, who were responsible for filming those first jumps—returned to El Capitan on September 9 to jump it themselves, along with four other jumpers, including two who jumped on the earlier outing. These jumps in the summer of 1978 set off a period of intense interest in El Capitan from the skydiving community. This was certainly helped by Boenish's concerted efforts to document these early jumps. His participation in and organization of many of these jumps, combined with this documentation, largely explains his positioning as the "father" of BASE jumping. This interest brought El Capitan to the attention of the United States Parachuting Association (USPA) Board of Directors (BOD). This interest was, in part at least, driven by the perception that El Capitan was the only cliff on earth that could safely be jumped. Again, this speaks to a degree of myopia, as other cliffs (e.g., in the Dolomites) not only *could* be jumped but *had* been jumped.

At their fall 1979 meeting, held in Arlington, Virginia, the USPA BOD officially adopted the following as its position on parachute jumps from fixed objects such as cliffs:

> USPA considers jumps using parachutes from fixed objects such as cliffs, buildings, and bridges to be stunts, much like those done for the movie industry. We recognize that the risks can be somewhat minimized, but such jumps may be significantly more dangerous than parachute jumps made from aircraft in accordance with the USPA Basic Safety Regulations.

This statement signaled a period of some unrest between skydiving and cliff jumping and perhaps set the stage for BASE jumping to eventually become a separate activity. Though many of the skydivers involved in early jumps from El Capitan were USPA members—some were even members of the BOD—the USPA and other skydiving organizations have been hesitant to embrace fixed-object jumping. As an organization with a mandate to promote and foster safe parachute jumping (obviously only part of their purpose), the USPA had little choice but to point out that fixed-object jumps are more dangerous than jumps from aircraft.

the national park service gets involved

The first evidence of National Park Service (NPS) involvement in cliff jumping in Yosemite came in September 1978; on Carl Boenish's first jump, he and his five companions were arrested. By Park Service estimates, there were 120 jumps between 1978 and 1980, though only 23 of these jumpers were caught. Perhaps frustrated by their inability to keep cliff jumpers from leaping from El Capitan, the NPS entered into discussions with the USPA to legalize jumping from "El Cap." Particularly key in these discussions was a seminar held in Perris Valley, California, in February of 1980. At this meeting a few dozen El Capitan enthusiasts (including Boenish), along with select members of the USPA BOD, met with YNP chief ranger Bill Wendt. Wendt, though obviously a key representative of the NPS, was also a former smoke jumper, and there is some evidence that he was generally quite supportive of a program to legalize (and, of course, regulate) jumping from El Capitan. Discussion at the meeting was first centered on whether jumps from El Capitan could be made within the parameters of USPA basic safety recommendations. Consensus was that they could not but that jumps could still be safely made from the peak by qualified jumpers. So the second part of the meeting was devoted to drafting a set of regulations and recommendations to ensure that jumps from El Capitan were safe and respected the needs and interests of the NPS and other park visitors.

Eventually, the committee issued a report outlining its recommendations. This report contained USPA recommendations, including a number of dimensions under the broad headings of "experience and ability," "equipment" (e.g., ram-air parachute only), "maximum winds," and "free-fall time" (between six and eight seconds for adequate separation from the wall and safe deployment altitude). It also, however, outlined NPS requirements, including specific launch and landing sites, mandatory support teams at both the launch and landing sites, time limits (time of day and time of year), and prohibitions on particular aerial maneuvers. Finally, the report outlined "approvals," indicating that permits were required both for the jump and for the hike to the exit point, and that only 12 jump permits would be issued for any particular day. It seemed, at this point, that there was a good degree of cooperation between jumpers and the NPS in organizing a program of jumping from El Capitan. For a brief period, at least, there was some common ground between these groups with somewhat different interests and agendas.

The regulations described were aimed at minimizing the impact of jumping on the park itself, maximizing the odds of good jumping conditions, and keeping the jumps from becoming a spectacle that would distract other park visitors. The conditions that were to be met in order to first qualify for, and later comply with, jumping permits were quite specific to the activity. These included a minimum level of certified competence in skydiving and a 30-second gap between jumpers to further enhance the safety of jumps. The first of these illustrates the blurring of boundaries, at this time, between skydiving and cliff jumping. The second was specifically aimed at preventing jumpers from engaging in what is sometimes called "relative work"—that is, jumpers in freefall in close proximity with one another. This requirement, it turned out, would become something of an issue.

The next step involved a demonstration jump being made on July 1, 1980, by the chair of the USPA El Capitan committee, Joe Svec, along with several other jumpers. After this demonstration, U.S. Fish and Wildlife Service officials decided that jumping was too potentially disruptive to a pair of peregrine falcons nesting on the cliff face and determined that jumping could not begin until August 1 that year. (In principle, the jumping season would begin after the Memorial Day weekend in future years.) Svec later recalled his involvement in the planning process for the program of jumping in Yosemite in an editorial written for a leading skydiving publication. In this piece, he points to the environmental vision of John Muir, one of the touchstone figures of the modern environmental movement. Muir, he said, "understands the beauty of the valley and the need for preserving it in its natural state for future generations. Muir's writings were always on my mind when I sat with Park Service personnel and discussed the opening of El Capitan for skydiving" (Svec 1980).

the best-laid plans

For the first week of August or thereabouts, jumping went more or less according to plans, with the Park Service issuing permits, jumpers generally abiding by the regulations and recommendations, and jumps taking place without serious incident (though there was one broken nose). After that time, though, there were a number of incidents—including some more serious injuries and various violations of the permit system—that caused the NPS to question the viability of the program. The most notable of these incidents occurred between August 26 and 30, 1980. First, on August 26, a group of seven skydivers, organized by Dennis Murphy, allegedly violated regulations by driving past a chained gate in order to shorten the hike to the peak and by attempting to perform relative work from El Capitan, launching as a group of three and a group of four. Murphy allegedly bragged about this later, suggesting that the group had demonstrated that jumpers could safely do relative work from the peak. Second, on August 30, the so-called "flatbed 10" allegedly helped pull back a log-and-rock barricade in order to continue driving on a closed road, again to shorten the hike. In part because of these transgressions, the program of legalized cliff jumps in Yosemite drew heavily on NPS resources, and the program was terminated on September 9.

At the same time, a number of jumpers were not impressed with either the NPS or the USPA. The NPS, in the opinion of some, was "abusive" of cliff jumpers in a number of respects. Robin Heid, director of the Wildlife Society, sent a number of letters in May of 1983 to Park Services and to elected officials, outlining these allegations. Drawing explicitly on a discourse of civil liberty, Heid suggests that the NPS had no intention of permitting jumping in Yosemite in the long term. Instead, he offers, the NPS pretended to cooperate with the USPA only to bring jumping squarely under its mandate, thus legitimating its authority to regulate—and prohibit—the activity. In addition, Heid suggests that the NPS program "had been *designed* by the NPS as both a managerial and a budgetary impossibility in order to 'prove' the activity's unviability in Yosemite Valley." In a recent interview, I mentioned Heid's allegation to Wendt, who said: "Oh, that's bullshit . . . [the jumping program] was pretty straightforward. We had a successful . . . hang-glider program. . . . It wasn't designed to fail at all; it was designed to succeed. [But] there were too many free spirits. That's the long and the short of it."

One important dimension of the program's demise was that the NPS indicated to the USPA that it expected the USPA to severely sanction its members who were involved in the infractions outlined above. The USPA wasted little time in doing so. Shortly after a meeting on September 13, 1980, it issued a memorandum to "USPA affiliated clubs, centers, and drop zones." This memorandum outlined sanctions against various members, including permanent expulsion from the organization of the Dennis Murphy group, along with one-year suspensions for the flatbed 10. The suspensions and expulsions, as well as the perceived lack of due process, were rather controversial. Several of the affected members, for example, wrote letters of appeal to the USPA. Some writers were contrite for what they called errors in judgment, apologizing to the USPA for their contributions to the demise of legalized jumping in Yosemite. Others were less apologetic in tone. Most, though, criticized the process by which the USPA arrived at these disciplinary actions. In a letter to the BOD, dated January 8, 1981, Michael Steele, a member of the Dennis Murphy group, stated:

> Could it be that the board members may have acted hastily in administering their judgement [*sic*]? And was the decision to revoke memberships of those involved reached as a possible bargaining measure to impress Park Officials for any future negotiations to reopen the Park to skydivers?

Cliff Chema, a member of the flatbed 10, also wrote a letter to the USPA BOD (undated), and went further in criticizing the USPA's actions:

> [Neither the] letter from the USPA asked me what happened nor did the Directors I talked to care what happened. I don't deny being with a group of people in Yosemite one of who [*sic*] received a misdemeanor

traffic violation. I strongly deny being the cause of termination of legal jumping off El Capp which USPA eleged [sic] and I refuse to lie down and be a victim of a USPA witch-hunt.

Some of these letters also raise allegations that Park Service staff were specifically targeting jumpers. In a letter to the USPA BOD dated January 13, 1981, Max Kelly, a member of the flatbed 10, noted,

While we were waiting at the entrance, the same rangers who [revoked] our permits allowed two civilian vehicles to pass the same road closed sign. We asked them why and they laughed at us and said that's the way it is. It was evident to me that the rangers were only after the jumpers.

This program of legalized cliff jumping in YNP also became the subject of some negative feedback from members of the public. For example, an August 12, 1980, letter from Michael Ann Rex to the director of the NPS (and copied to senators Henry Jackson and Gary Hart) reads, in part:

How can you allow an infinitesimal number of people to desecrate this regal, beautiful monument? Do you think nothing will be harmed, trees won't be broken, animals not disturbed[?] Yosemite is a natural area, not a recreation area. Its beauty has been preserved to allow generations to enjoy *nature*, . . . to assist them in enjoying it and the wilderness and everything that is special about that. Instead, it is being turned into a CIRCUS!

The NPS position was that it would be better to have jumping that was regulated, monitored, and controlled than to continue to have jumping that was under the radar, costly to police, and much more difficult to ensure that it met reasonable standards of safety and care. As the superintendent of Yosemite wrote in an October 1980, response to Rex,

When requests [like those of the parachutists seeking to jump from El Capitan] are received by members of the park staff, they are weighed on the basis of whether they will result in damage to park resources, jeopardize the safety of park visitors, create a spectacle, cause undue demand on limited staff time, or unacceptably disturb park visitors.

This (brief) period of legalized jumping in Yosemite, and the exchanges from the years that followed, captures the tensions both within the skydiving and BASE jumping communities and between jumpers, the

Park Service, and the public more generally. These tensions continue to manifest themselves, as I explore in subsequent chapters.

from cliff jumping to BASE

The period of the 1960s to late 1970s is a critical one in terms of the development of BASE. Small groups of skydivers in different geographical areas seemed to be working towards a common aim, though without necessarily having much knowledge of each other or formal organization between groups. The early 1980s would mark an important shift in this regard. It is in this period that we witness perhaps the most important contributions of Carl Boenish and his colleagues. Boenish was not unique in endeavoring to solve the technical difficulties associated with parachuting from a fixed object. He was not even the only person endeavoring to document these early jumps on film, as evidenced by *Sensation Alpen,* filmed over a decade before Boenish did his first jump from El Capitan. Where Boenish really illustrated his passion—what really marks him as a visionary—is his influence in organizing a previously haphazard activity (at the broad level) into a relatively coherent and cohesive one with practitioners who shared both technical information and a relatively coherent vision of the subculture and of BASE as an activity unto itself.

Much of the activity described above took place in the months and years following the contentious summer of 1980 in Yosemite. Early in 1981, Boenish, along with his wife Jean, Phil Smith, and Phil Mayfield, set out to come up with an acronym that would serve as the name for this new activity. They debated a number of options before settling on the term *BASE.* Also around this time, they proposed that once a jumper had jumped at least one object in each of the four categories, they would qualify for a "BASE number." After jumping from a Houston skyscraper in January, 1981, Smith and Mayfield were awarded BASE numbers 1 and 2, respectively (each had already jumped objects in the other three categories). The moments before this notable jump were described as follows in the pages of *Texas Monthly*:

At precisely 8:15 on the chilly, overcast morning of January 18, 1981, Phillip Hammond Smith perched on the 72nd floor of the still unfinished Texas Commerce Tower in Houston and prepared to jump. Smith, a lean but hard-muscled five feet ten inches tall, was dressed in a billowing red jump suit, an orange parachute harness, a white Bell

> **The first BASE number (achieved by jumping from objects in each of the four main categories) was issued in 1981. By 1986, there had been approximately 100 BASE numbers issued.**

crash helmet with two backward-pointing cameras mounted on it, and a pair of aviator-style prescription glasses. (Hurt 1981, 178)

Smith had spent months checking out the tower as it was under construction, visiting it several times to research access, the exit, and wind conditions aloft. On the morning of the jump itself, all was going according to plan. "Smitty" and Mayfield were in position, as was their crew, including Carl and Jean Boenish and a number of people dedicated to capturing the event on film:

All of a sudden, a yellow-and-brown striped Bell Jet Ranger helicopter came out of the patchy sky and began orbiting the tower on a 75-foot radius. On the second pass, one of the passengers waved at Smitty, signaling that the helicopter-borne-photographers were ready. . . . Since jumping the Texas Commerce Tower had been Smitty's idea, he intended to be the first to go off, a distinction that would qualify him as BASE No. 1. (Hurt 1981, 183)

The next weekend, on January 24, 1981, Jean and Carl Boenish qualified for BASE numbers 3 and 4, respectively, after jumping the same tower with Smith and Mayfield. From 1981 to the present day, BASE numbers have continued to be issued, though this has been administered by different jumpers at different times. As of the time of writing, there were upwards of 1,400 BASE numbers issued. It should be noted, though, that not every jumper who qualifies for a BASE number applies for one.

Boenish's other important contribution during this time was the institution of a magazine to promote the safety of BASE jumping and information sharing. *BASE Magazine* accomplished both of these aims and as a consequence played a pivotal role in the institutionalization of a sport that was, until then, basically either a stunt activity or an offshoot of skydiving. According to the *Texas Monthly* article, *BASE Magazine*

featured a logo that could be worn by those who had jumped in all four categories, as well as statistics on all recorded BASE jumps, how-to articles by experienced BASE jumpers, and reprints of various newspaper stories pro and con fixed-object jumping. Although he nodded to commercialism by running ads for his Photo-Chuting Enterprises, Boenish took care not to neglect the philosophical basis of BASE. . . . the overall BASE ideology was summarized by an unattributed quote Boenish had found on a wall at a skydiving center in Florida. Listed among *BASE Magazine's* "Quotations to Inspire us By," the passage began with the sentence "I do not choose to be a common man." (Hurt 1981, 301)

This "unattributed quote," it turns out, is from labor leader Dean Alfange's "To Be an American." It is perhaps fitting as a piece of literature informing the philosophy of BASE, as decades earlier it had been cited in discussions of the philosophy of climbing in the Yosemite valley (Taylor 2010, 138).

legal issues continue

The summer of 1980 would by no means represent the end of the struggle over the legalization of BASE. In Yosemite, jumpers continued to push for a program of permitted jumping in the park for a number of years. And in the absence of such a program, many jumpers simply continued jumping, knowing that if they were caught they would likely be charged, have their gear confiscated, and often face a significant fine. Jumping continued in the park to such an extent as to justify having a position (or, often, more than one) specifically dedicated to anticipating and monitoring jumping activities and attempting to catch "perpetrators" in the act. I spoke with Daniel Horner, who was in the position of special agent— what he called "basically a criminal investigator" for the United States federal government—in the mid-1990s (though he had been working in the Yosemite Valley since 1983). The focus of his job was on preventing and policing BASE jumping in the park, and it involved, among other things, paying close attention to website "chatter" in order to anticipate jumps that were in the planning stages. As he said, his "whole involvement in it was on the enforcement side. I was never involved in being a policy setter. . . . I was a cop." He also informed me that he and his staff relied on reports from rock climbers, many of whom frequented El Capitan and other peaks in the park, in their efforts to catch and charge BASE jumpers. This offers some illustration of the kinds of resources devoted to the policing of BASE jumping in YNP.

In October 1999, BASE jumping in Yosemite was once again in the news as a small group of jumpers organized a protest jump in the park, in part spurred by the allegedly heavy-handed tactics of park staff in policing the activity (allegations, it should be noted, that Horner flatly denies). The protest jump itself may or may not have generated much media interest. Sadly, though, it became a story when Jan Davis, one of the jumpers, died. Knowing that her gear would be confiscated, Davis opted not to use her usual rig, instead using one that she could afford to lose to the authorities. The rig Davis elected to use had a slightly different configuration, one that was less familiar to her. Whether because of this configuration issue or for some other reason, Davis failed to activate her parachute before impact. Adding to an already tragic set of circumstances was the fact that Davis' husband, filmmaker Tom Sanders, was filming the protest jumps, including that of his wife.

The legality of BASE continues to be an issue, for a host of reasons. Though jumping itself is generally not illegal, jumpers, if caught, are often cited for other violations, including trespassing and public endangerment, to name just two. This is particularly the case for urban jumps, which tend to be more difficult to conceal and require more stealth in terms of an escape. Though some jumpers have little interest in these kinds of jumps, others are drawn to them, either because of the nature of the object or, in some cases, for the thrill of trying to evade the law. Jeb Corliss, for example, was caught trying to jump the Empire State Building in New York in 2006. Corliss had concealed his gear under a "fat suit" as he gained access to the viewing area. He went to the washroom, shed the fat suit, donned his rig, then tried to scale a wall for his jump. He was caught by a security guard, and a struggle ensued before Corliss was apprehended. Not only did this jump bring Corliss some notoriety, but some said that it brought negative attention to the sport and called it a violation of BASE ethics.

That said, there are a number of jumps and events that are perfectly legal, including those for which temporary permits are acquired (e.g., Bridge Day), some that are legal year-round (e.g., the Perrine Bridge in Twin Falls, Idaho), and others that are simply not violations of local legislation (see Cooper and Laurendeau 2007). For example, the Bureau of Land Management seems to be relatively friendly towards jumping, as is the case in Utah. I consider some of these sites in greater detail in Chapter 5.

In the last three decades, a number of important technical advances have shaped the development of BASE. This began in the mid-1980s with the development of BASE-specific gear. The most recent developments in

BASE include the advent of the wingsuit and the various dimensions of the activity opened up by this new technology. Wingsuits allow jumpers to slow their vertical fall rate substantially and also to increase their ability to cover distance horizontally. Taken together, this has set the stage for both proximity flying and for projects like Jeb Corliss's "landing project." I consider each of these technical developments in greater detail in the following chapters.

5. techniques and equipment

in certain respects, the modern-day practice of BASE jumping bears little resemblance to the jumps that laid the foundations of the modern activity in the late 1970s. This is particularly so with respect to equipment. Initially, jumpers had little choice but to use skydiving gear in their exploits. Moreover, because of the nature of skydiving and skydiving equipment at the time, most, if not all, of these early jumpers were experts about their gear. This is not necessarily the case now, in large part because of the dramatic changes in both skydiving and BASE in the intervening 30 years. In the 1970s and 1980s, though, parachuting technology was changing so dramatically that jumpers had to know their gear "inside-out," as the saying goes. These were the early years of the transition from "rounds" (a term used to refer broadly to refer to round canopies) to "squares" (referring to rectangular and elliptical canopies) and beyond. This transition did not, of course, happen overnight. As jumpers built on their foundation of knowledge about the flight characteristics (and limitations!) of round canopies, they became familiar with ParaCommander, and, eventually, with canopies designed with airplane wing technology explicitly in mind. This allowed for much greater maneuverability in the air and ultimately made it possible to jump into much tighter, less forgiving spaces. The next generation of skydiving canopies, though, has not had as much influence on BASE canopy technologies. As BASE-specific gear was developed, the two markets went in different directions; (most) skydiving canopies became faster, more maneuverable, and smaller, while BASE canopies remained about the same size and speed but became more stable and predictable, even in cases of object strike.

basic terms

In order to understand the various elements of BASE techniques and equipment, a bit of background is necessary on the technology informing contemporary skydiving equipment. A "rig" is generally composed of a container/harness system, as well as one or, in the case of skydiving, two canopies. Modern canopies are designed based on similar principles as those that inform airplane wing technology. A wing is "trimmed" (the lines leading to the front—the nose—of the canopy are slightly shorter than those leading to the rear—the tail—of the canopy) to have a particular "angle of attack." It is this angle of attack that determines how steeply a given canopy will descend. Perhaps the most important difference between modern rectangular canopies and older technologies (e.g., "rounds") is their maneuverability. Round canopies, to a large extent, are at the mercy of the wind. Canopy pilots certainly have some control over their direction simply by turning their canopy. Rounds generate such low forward speed, though, that this control has serious limits.

"Squares" (though this is what they're often called, modern canopies more closely resemble rectangles) represent a significant improvement over rounds in terms of maneuverability. Each canopy is composed of a number of cells, each of which is open at the nose and closed at the tail. Each cell is designed to remain inflated during flight, such that even in a case where one or two outside cells fails to inflate (canopies inflate from the center to the outside during the deployment sequence), the canopy will still fly relatively well. Most BASE canopies have seven cells. Attached to the two outside cells are steering lines or brake lines. As a jumper pulls on the brake line on a given side, the tail of that outside cell is cupped somewhat, creating drag (and a degree of lift as well). When that happens, that side of the canopy flies more slowly than the other side, creating a turn in the canopy. (In the case of an aggressive turn, there is also a noticeable "dive" as the canopy turns because the side "in brakes" has more lift than the other.) The net result of this is that canopies are extremely maneuverable, making it possible for experienced jumpers to navigate to specific and precise landing areas with relative ease. As a jumper comes in to land, he or she pulls on both brake lines at the same time, converting forward speed into lift and drag on both sides, thus slowing the parachute's descent and resulting in a relatively soft landing (when done properly).

The deployment system of a BASE rig is quite similar to that of a skydiving rig and is perhaps even more important than in skydiving. In

> While most BASE-specific canopies have seven cells, the majority of canopies used in recreational skydiving have nine. In general, skydiving canopies are slightly faster and more responsive to input than are BASE canopies. Because of this, though, they're less well suited for the particular demands of BASE.

skydiving, a jumper has a great deal of open space at opening (or should), so an off-heading opening, in which the parachute opens facing a different direction than the jumper, is not critical, generally speaking. In BASE, however, off-heading openings can result in serious injury or death, depending on the situation. One of my interviewees, for example, had an off-heading opening when jumping from a cliff, so his parachute flew him immediately back into the face of the mountain from which he had just jumped. Object strike is perhaps the most serious hazard in BASE, depending on the particular kind of jump in question, so the deployment system of a BASE rig is designed to ensure "clean" openings. In the case of a freefall jump, when a jumper is ready to deploy his or her chute, he or she tosses a "pilot chute" away from his or her body. A pilot chute is in

A BASE jumper under a seven-cell canopy. The pilot chut (blue) trails behind. (Shariff Che' Lah/Dreamstime.com)

effect a miniature parachute. It creates drag and is attached to both the container/harness system and to the main canopy (the only canopy, in the case of BASE rigs). As the pilot chute drags behind the falling jumper, it opens the container (which might be closed by pins or by Velcro, depending on the design), then extracts the canopy in such a way as to provide the best conditions for a clean, on-heading opening. It is difficult to overstate the importance of the pilot chute in the deployment sequence. If the pilot chute does not find "clean air" (if it is tossed into the "burble" created by a falling object—the jumper—it will not create drag and will not open the container and extract the parachute). Obviously, in the case of a system with only one canopy, the result would be disastrous. How one tosses the pilot chute is also important, as any forces on it as it creates drag will be passed along through the rest of the deployment sequence. If it is spinning as it drags behind a jumper, that rotation is passed along through the bridle to the parachute, potentially resulting in "line twists," a situation where a canopy is at least partially inflated but the lines between the canopy and the jumper are twisted. This makes the canopy difficult—if not impossible—to steer or land well and also increases the rate of descent of the canopy. Obviously, this is not a desirable situation. Again, in skydiving, this is generally not disastrous, as a jumper generally has minutes to clear the twists, fly to the landing zone, and land safely. BASE jumps, and particularly those from very low altitudes, are another story. Often, a jumper deploys her or his canopy at such a low altitude that line twists would mean that a parachute would not fully inflate or could not be steered prior to impact with the earth.

Another factor to consider in the opening sequence is the speed of the opening. Depending on the height of the object and the length of the delay, a jumper may want a very fast opening or a much slower one. A fast opening is beneficial, even necessary, in the case of very low objects. In this case, there is simply not enough time for a canopy to open softly (slowly). In the case of higher objects, though, and especially if a jumper is planning to free-fall for a time prior to deployment, a fast opening is often undesirable, as it would decelerate a jumper much too quickly and potentially result in injury. The primary mechanism for adjusting the speed of the opening is the slider. A slider is a piece of material that runs along the four main line groups of a parachute (each line group runs through its own grommet). When it is packed in the "up" position (hence the term "slider up jump"), it holds the line groups together somewhat, slowing the opening. As the canopy starts to inflate, the pressure of the outer cells inflating forces the slider down the lines towards the risers that attach the lines to the container/harness system. This slows (and softens) the opening sequence. So, when a jumper wishes to have a fast opening, she or he packs the slider down at or near the risers, essentially removing this effect from the opening sequence.

As BASE has developed, so too has the gear and equipment associated with the activity. As is the case in skydiving, gear manufacturers are always looking for ways to improve their products, whether the improvements have to do with safety (first and foremost) or comfort. Two recent examples will illustrate this idea. Some time after the development of BASE-specific canopies, the search for ways to improve them continued. As mentioned above, one of the main hazards of BASE is object strike. This is a problem not only because a jumper could be hurt in colliding with an object but because this has the potential to "shut down" a parachute as well. The forward drive of the parachute would cease, even if only briefly, meaning air would no longer be forced into the nose of the canopy. Many square canopies would deflate in these conditions, and there would be little to prevent a jumper from essentially returning to freefall as the canopy worked to reinflate.

Two important developments in canopy technology aimed to address the problem described above as well as to improve other flight characteristics particularly relevant to BASE jumpers. These developments are known as valves and vents (see http://www.basejumper.com/Articles/Gear/BASE _Canopies_681.html, accessed July 27, 2011). Vents are located on the underside of the canopy, often near the nose. They assist in faster deployment of a parachute by forcing air onto the underside of the top of the canopy. As a result, they minimize the time between the bottom of the canopy "catching air" and the top of the canopy inflating. The result is that the canopy is flying (and controllable) sooner. This is particularly important in terms of avoiding object strike in the case of an off-heading opening. The second main benefit to vents is that they help keep the canopy inflated in circumstances where there is not much forward speed (one of my interviewees struck a cliff face, and his vented canopy remained inflated as he lost altitude along the cliff face). In the earliest days of vented canopies, there were some problems with canopies depressurizing as air escaped through the same vents by which it had entered. This often resulted in reduced performance (especially a weaker flare) of the canopy. The introduction of valves addressed this problem by allowing air to enter the canopy but preventing it from escaping.

A number of other developments related to equipment and packing techniques are aimed at improving the safety of BASE. For example, jumpers commonly use a "tailgate," described on an online forum devoted to packing issues as follows:

> Early in the development of BASE-specific canopies, it was noted that the rear corners of the canopy frequently "inverted" themselves during slider-down openings. Most often, these tail inversions would clear themselves before the canopy was fully inflated. Sometimes, however, they would develop into a line over malfunction [where one or more lines sit over top of a partially inflated canopy, preventing full inflation, and often making the canopy difficult to control]. The tailgate helps to promote nose-first inflation by delaying the deployment and inflation of the rear of the canopy. It very significantly reduces (but does not eliminate) the incidence of line overs on Slider Down or Slider Off jumps. (http://www.blincmagazine.com/forum/wiki/Tailgate, accessed July 27, 2011)

One other example is that jumpers are taught to put their hands on their rear risers as soon as possible after opening (even during the opening sequence). Parachutes respond to riser input more quickly than to steering line input, and this takes less time for jumpers as well. So, in the event that a jumper senses an off-heading opening, he or she can initiate a correction as soon as possible to avoid object strike.

As noted above, the term *BASE* is an acronym for Building, Antenna (or "aerial"), Span (i.e., bridges), Earth (i.e., cliffs and other rock formations)— the four representative types of object from which participants jump. While not all objects immediately fall into one of these four categories, it's common to place objects in one of these four classes according to wind interaction and structural features as an aid to assessing risks. For other purposes, objects that don't neatly fit one of these categories may simply be designated "Other." For example, most jumpers would classify a structure as a building only if it were meant to be occupied. When launching from taller objects, jumpers might go through a short freefall before opening their parachutes. When jumping from shorter objects, though, a jumper might set up a "static line," which would open the parachute right after the jump.

"pushing the envelope": jumping techniques and aerial maneuvers

What I have described above captures the basic elements of what some might refer to as routine BASE jumps. As a number of researchers have documented in other "lifestyle sports," as practitioners gain experience and skill, they often "up the ante," taking on dimensions of the activity that require more skill and experience. Though these dimensions may seem to increase the risk of the activity in an objective sense, this ignores the fact that what constitutes a risk is relative to participants' skill level as well as their ability to make sound judgments as to whether a particular BASE jump (in this case) is within their capabilities under the circumstances. The case of James described in Chapter 1 (where he stood down from a "runner") is a case in point. James is a fairly experienced jumper and is certainly well past the stage of simply doing routine jumps. In fact, he and another jumper spent a good deal of time several years ago "pushing the envelope" in terms of doing extremely low-altitude jumps. In his interview, he described one of the lowest (110 feet) as follows:

> The first time we jumped [a particular bridge] was really intense. . . . George and I had jumped something that was 130 feet before, but we really weren't sure, exactly, about 110. We knew the canopy would open but we just weren't sure how far the impact to the bottom would be. And so there was a lot of preparation behind that one and as we came up on the jump, George decided he didn't want to do it, because he had a trip coming up and didn't want broken legs.
>
> I decided to go for it anyway and it was just, I remember, I mean, I remember standing on the bridge and looking down at [my ground crew] in the landing area. And it was like, like standing here looking at you. I could see their eyes very clearly. And If I wanted to talk to them I could just talk to them like this. But at the same time we had done so much preparation before hand on that one. That's one of these ones where I actually feel like that one was grounded in a really good place. . . . But when I landed it was just like, I don't know, I just wanted to hug everybody and I remember for sure, I remember Dave's video from the bridge and I can't remember exactly what he said. But just after I jumped, there was just this comment on the video that was something along the lines of "Holy Shit!" Because it was just, because nobody was exactly sure quite how that one was going to go.

It is illustrative, then, both that James has "pushed the envelope" in this way and that he stood down from the cliff jump (and, it should be noted, others) later in his career. The point is that he (and most jumpers with whom I spoke) do not add in elements just for the sake of doing so. Instead, they carefully consider how current they are, what the conditions (e.g., wind, light) are, and whether or not this is the time to push the envelope in a particular way. On the same jump where James decided to stand down, for example, the first two jumpers performed runners from this 300-foot cliff. The third jumper to go, feeling especially comfortable with this jump (and current on runners) strode up to the cliff's edge quite calmly and did a backflip as he launched. This illustrates another way in which some jumpers push the envelope: by doing an aerial maneuver prior to activating their parachute. Many of the films produced by and for jumpers, whether they're commercially available circulated electronically, document jumpers doing spectacular aerial maneuvers as they launch from an object. Furthermore, some jumpers (e.g., Jeb Corliss) are particularly well known for their skill at aerials.

wingsuits

The 1990s marked an important era, both in BASE and in skydiving, as a number of jumpers worked to create a wingsuit—a jumpsuit that makes jumpers resemble a flying squirrel somewhat. The idea is that by wearing this suit, a jumper can significantly slow his or her fall rate and, at the same time, increase the horizontal speed generated. Prior to the advent of the wingsuits, this had been simply a function of a jumper's ability to "track" (a maneuver involving de-arching, extending the legs, and sweeping the arms back). In 1999, Jari Kuosma and Robert Pečnik created, manufactured, and distributed a wingsuit, in the process establishing a company named BirdMan, Inc. Kuosma and Pečnik did more than design and manufacture the equipment; they also advocated that wingsuits could be used safely (in the early years of their development, wingsuits carried quite a stigma for being too dangerous). As part of this project, they developed an instructor program. Other people and organizations have since developed similar programs.

To further explain wingsuit technology, a scenario is in order. A jumper enters freefall (initially, these jumps were all made from aircraft) wearing both a wingsuit and a skydiving rig. The jumper then "flies" the wingsuit on what is known in skydiving (and, to a lesser extent, BASE jumping) as the "relative wind." This term refers not to wind per se but to the air movement relative to a jumper. So, at the time of leaving an aircraft, for example, the relative wind is from the nose of the aircraft to its tail, as the aircraft is, of course, flying forward. As a jumper bleeds off the forward throw of the aircraft, though, the relative wind transitions and "comes up" from below. (Of course, the wind is not coming up; the jumper is falling through air.

A 2010 wingsuit jump at Kjerag, Norway. (Evgeniya Moroz/Dreamstime.com)

Nevertheless, the perception is that there is wind from below, and this is what's important in terms of flying one's body or a wingsuit.) At a predetermined altitude, the jumper deploys his or her parachute and lands, still wearing the wingsuit. (As I describe in Chapters 7 and 8, though, some jumpers are determined to land a wingsuit without deploying a parachute).

"Flying" a wingsuit is much like "flying" one's body in freefall. The wingsuit flier adjusts body position in order to generate lift, resulting in the ability to cover great distances horizontally (if this lift is evenly applied to both sides) and create turns (if the lift is applied more to one side than another). As noted on an online wingsuit forum,

A pilot can choose to manipulate his fall rate towards Earth with the goal of achieving the slowest vertical speed in order to prolong time in freefall, or the pilot can try to maximize the horizontal glide distance across the Earth. The pilot manipulates these flight characteristics by changing the shape of his torso, arching or bending at the shoulders, hips, and knees, and by changing the angle of attack in which the wingsuit flies in the relative wind, and by the amount of tension applied to the fabric wings of the suit. (http://forums.wtf.com/threads/wingsuits-the-only-way-to-fly.38833/, accessed July 27, 2011)

Though wingsuits were initially developed primarily by jumpers involved in skydiving, their implications for BASE jumpers soon became obvious. For the experienced wingsuit flier, the wingsuit dramatically improves the ability to generate separation between oneself and hazards (including the object from which one is jumping). That said, the use to which many jumpers are now putting wingsuit is rather different. Instead of maximizing the space between themselves and hazards, many jumpers are now using the maneuverability of wingsuits to get as close as possible to hazards, flying within feet of canyon walls, for example. This activity is known as proximity flying and represents perhaps the leading edge of BASE in the years ahead.

6. sites and events

in a technical sense, BASE jumpers can undertake their activity almost anywhere. Though I outline the touchstone locations and objects in this section, this is in certain respects rather misleading. One of the aims of BASE jumpers, particularly those on the cutting edge of the activity, is to do something that has never before been done. In that sense, locations like the Perrine Bridge, or even El Capitan, are rather run of the mill (though the jumps themselves may not be!). Especially when we take into account the spiritual element of BASE that I mentioned in Chapter 1, it is no surprise that for many jumpers the most interesting jumps—or at least those in which they invest the most time and energy—are those that involve "opening" a new location. These are unlikely to appear on a list of sites and events in a book such as this one. "Hardcore" jumpers are likely to take just as much, if not more, pleasure in jumps that are new to them, or, better yet, new to BASE jumping. A recent expedition by a number of jumpers from different countries to Baffin Island, in the Canadian Arctic Archipelago, illustrates this idea. For those who took part in this adventure, a large part of the thrill was in encountering and working to overcome the challenges associated with jumping new objects in conditions that were not always favorable.

el capitan

Located in Yosemite National Park (YNP) in Central California, El Capitan ("El Cap") is a touchstone location for BASE jumping. Though I discussed El Cap in detail in Chapter 4, it bears briefly revisiting in this section, given its importance in a number of different respects. El Cap is a picturesque object that has long been popular with rock climbers, hikers, and paragliders, among others. It is also, however, one of the most important locations to understand in terms of the history of BASE jumping. It

El Capitan, in California's Yosemite National Park, is the site of a number of the most iconic jumps in the history of BASE. (Dreamstime.com)

was here that some of the most important early jumps were made, including those by Mike Pelkey and Brian Schubert in 1966 and by Carl Boenish and several other jumpers in the late 1970s. It was also at El Cap that an important struggle over the legalization of BASE—if only in national parks—took place. This period in 1980 also went a long way towards the establishment of BASE as an activity with a separate ethos from that of skydiving. BASE developed into its own activity in part because of the efforts of some of these early jumpers—especially Carl Boenish—but the tensions that developed between cliff jumpers and the skydiving community around the program of permitted jumping in YNP in 1980 are also important to understand in this respect. El Capitan continues to be a touchstone object in the BASE community, and jumpers continue to make pilgrimage to the site despite the prohibition against jumping there.

bridge day

At 876 feet high, the New River Gorge Bridge in West Virginia is one of the highest vehicular bridges in the world. Jumping is forbidden there with the exception of one day a year as it lies within the New River Gorge

The New River Gorge Bridge in Fayetteville, West Virginia, is the site of Bridge Day festivities. (Dreamstime.com)

National River Park. Each year, however, from 9:00 a.m. to 3:00 p.m. on the third Saturday in October, BASE jumping is legal and formally sanctioned. The event has been held every year (except 2001, owing to the events of 9/11) from 1980 to the present. Bridge Day attracts more than 450 BASE jumpers and 200,000 spectators annually.

Like Matthew (see Chapter 2), a number of prospective jumpers make their first BASE jumps at Bridge Day. For one thing, bridges are generally the safest object type in terms of avoiding object strike. More specifically, though, the height of the New River Gorge Bridge makes it a relatively safe object, and organizers also ensure that there are boats available to pull jumpers from the river after water landings. As Matthew said, "With an army of ambulances, there's a river you can land in, they'll pick you up if you freak out, have canopy issues, or . . . It's a really good spot to start." Though in certain respects this sounds ideal, some jumpers are somewhat critical of Bridge Day in the sense that the "bar is set too low." Because of the popularity of the event and the relative safety of the object, they fear that jumpers who have neither adequate training nor a serious commitment to the sport consider it an opportunity to come and do a BASE jump, if only to say that they have done one.

In the following field note, written during my first-jump course, I further illustrate the potential hazards of Bridge Day:

> Today, on the last day of the course, Cam reminded me of the dangers of the sport with a number of videos. Perhaps the one that stuck with me the most was a Bridge Day video, showing jumper after jumper exiting the bridge, and a number of landings. Though I'm not an expert at this point, even I could see that many of the launches were dangerous, with jumpers going head-low before deploying their parachutes. Similarly, a number of jumpers did terrible approaches to the landing area. In some cases, this was not a costly mistake, as they simply landed in the water. In others, though, ill-advised low turns resulted in sprained ankles, broken legs, and one broken back. Cam seems to show this film as part of his course in order to remind his students not to be complacent; even if a jump looks straightforward, you have to be on your game. (August 2007)

Over the years, there have been two fatalities at Bridge Day. Though some argue that this is a relatively good record in light of how long Bridge Day has been going on, others point out that this is a somewhat high number considering that the bridge is only jumped one day a year.

One additional note about Bridge Day is worth mentioning here. Sociologists Jeff Ferrell, Stephen Lyng, and Dragan Milovanovic (2001) conducted a theoretical ethnography of Bridge Day and argue that the mediation of jumps is as important as the jumps themselves. Bridge Day jumps are filmed—both formally and informally—and many are relived in the minutes, hours, and weeks that follow. This mediation of jumps contributes to what these researchers call the "elongation of meaning." That is, the jumps are meaningful in and of themselves, but their meaning is also (re)constructed each time the jump is shown again, both in how it is presented and in the audience reaction to it.

twin falls

The community of Twin Falls, Idaho, has welcomed BASE jumpers as a part of its tourist industry. The Perrine Bridge, at 486 feet high, is legal to jump year-round, provided jumpers inform local authorities as to when jumping will begin and end on a given day. The Perrine Bridge is among the safest locations in North America. The Snake River moves slowly below the bridge, and a large meadow is available as a primary landing area. As such, this serves as a popular spot for jumpers to undertake at least some of their training. The safety and accessibility of the Perrine Bridge has also contributed to jumpers generally having higher numbers of jumps to their credit, with numerous jumpers having logged upwards of a quarter of their total jumps at this site.

norway

Jumpers from all over the world visit the fjords of southern Norway, some considering it a pilgrimage of sorts. Numerous cliffs measure over 2,000 feet, and the scree slopes below present numerous landing options. Together, this sets the stage for lengthy freefalls, even for some jumpers who do not have BASE-specific gear. At one site, jumpers can take advantage of camping near the cliffs, bus rides to the trailhead, boat rides back, and even an annual "heli-boogie" for jumpers who wish to forgo the two-hour hike.

In addition to being on many jumpers' "must-do" lists, Norway's sheer cliffs also have the distinction of having ended the jumping careers of a number of BASE jumpers—some of the biggest names in the sport among them. Perhaps most famously, Carl Boenish died on a jump in Norway.

kuala lumpur, malaysia

Recently, Malaysian officials have courted BASE jumpers as part of an effort to market their country as a tourist destination. Starting in 1999, the Malaysian government sanctioned jumps from structures such as the 1,483-foot Petronas towers in downtown Kuala Lumpur. In the years since, formalized BASE events have become somewhat institutionalized, as described on an extreme sports website:

> The first Base Jumping event to be held in Malaysia was on 1st February 2001. 50 jumpers took off from the Menara Kuala Lumpur completing 434 jumps inline with the Federal Territory Day celebrations in Kuala Lumpur. The event gained recognition from around the world and was the first major Base jumping event off a building to be hosted by any country. There are now many base jumping events being held in Malaysia attracting tourists and international base jumpers from around the globe.
>
> In 2008, The Kuala Lumpur International Base Jump Merdeka Circuit 2008 included six buildings from five different states in Malaysia. 40 international and 10 local base jumpers participated at the event, completing over 1200 jumps in three weeks. The buildings were the Menara Pelita in Sarawak, Menara Tun Mustapha in Sabah, Menara Alor Setar in Kehah, Menara Komtar in Penang, Menara in Kuala Lumpur and Menara Telekom Malaysia.
>
> Many tourists come to witness this event eagerly anticipating the base jumpers's to leap off the top of the buildings. The event provides the tourists with a chance to see many of the prominent buildings in Malaysia. Each visitor is attached to safety cables on the deck of the towers for safety and security reasons. Visitors wanting to make their stay can find the Citrus Hotel Kula Lumpur useful. The Citrus Hotel Kula Lumpur is a Discount Hotel in Kuala Lumpur. (http:// greatextremesports.com/view/80574/Base_Jumping_in_Malaysia, accessed July 27, 2011)

Even more recently, Malaysia has served as host for a number of high-profile BASE events, including the World BASE Cup, a world record for the most jumps in 24 hours (on December 31, 2005, Australian BASE jumper Gary Cunningham completed 133 jumps), and numerous others. In September and October 2011, 88 jumpers from 22 countries took part in KL Tower BASE Jump 2011, celebrating the 15th anniversary of the KL Tower (see http://www.kltowerjump.com/, accessed March 25, 2012).

Malaysia's Petronas Towers. (Dreamstime.com)

(other) exotic locations

It is perhaps unsurprising that in an activity in some sense organized around flouting convention, many jumpers enjoy jumping from objects that are in some sense unusual. Though these sites demand a good deal in the way of financial resources (not to mention time, specialized equipment, and so on), these kinds of sites draw numerous jumpers with some regularity. Examples include organized trips to Angel Falls, Venezuela; expeditions to Canada's Baffin Island; and (until jumps there were prohibited in early 2004) even Mexico's Cave of the Swallows, in which the entire freefall is made underground.

Other exotic locations have served as important sites in films about BASE. Recently, *Journey to the Center*, an award-winning entry in the Banff Mountain Film Festival, documented an expedition by three of the world's most renowned BASE jumpers (Chris McDougall, Jeb Corliss, and Paul Fortun) to jump Tian Keng near Chongqing, China. Known as the "Heavenly Pit," Tian Keng is a deep cavern with steep slopes and rocky terrain—logistically, a tremendously challenging jump. Add to that the fact that in order to access Tian Keng as a BASE jump, McDougall, Corliss, and Fortun had to pull themselves into the middle of the cavern along a suspended wire (leaving them tremendously exposed along the way), and it is easy to see why this site served as the focal point for the film.

world BASE race

The latest, and perhaps most high-profile, project that illustrates the ways in which BASE is becoming mainstream (in certain respects, at least) is the World BASE Race (WBR), held each year in Norway. The WBR is the brainchild of Norwegian jumper Paul Fortun. As the WBR website outlines, the race involves "two mountain flyers [BASE jumpers using wingsuit technology] navigating a mapped and measured distance towards a finish line. Upon finishing they deploy their parachutes and land safely." The race proceeds in heats, with the winner of each heat progressing to the next level of the competition. After a number of heats (the number depends on the number of entrants), the winner of the final race is crowned "the world's fastest flying human being" and receives the £3,000 first prize. Ronny Risvik claimed this title in the inaugural competition in 2008, Frode Johannessen won the competition in 2009, and Espen Fadnes took the 2010 title. Most recently, Frode Johannessen repeated his 2009 success, claiming the 2011 title as the "world's fastest flying human being."

In an interview prior to the 2009 event, Fortun shared his excitement about the event and the concept itself:

We have the world's most amazing public sporting event, in an arena located among the beautiful surroundings of nature itself. There is no registration fee for jumpers, or fee for public spectators. We want to make this the greatest public party for athletes and spectators alike. This event demonstrates to the world the type of athletes BASE jumpers truly are in an exciting competition. This is a top skilled athletic sport, where you not only have to compete head to head, but perform in front of the public. All rounds have to be hiked by the athletes, therefore the winner must also be in great physical shape.

The WBR illustrates that even an activity that is not especially well known, and is sometimes clandestine, is subject to the same market forces to become media friendly or at least create events that can be marketed in this way. Fortun notes, "This is a new sport, where the generations will study, make innovations and progress in the future. . . . Remember downhill skiing in the 1950's and look at where it is today, we are just getting started" (http://www.basejumper.com/Articles/Interviews_and_Profiles/ The_World_BASE_Race_Event_Featuring_Brendan_Nicholson_861 .html, accessed March 25, 2012).

BASE jump extreme world championship

Though a number of BASE competitions have been instituted in recent years, perhaps the most prestigious is the BASE Jump Extreme World Championship (initially known as World BASE Cup). Inaugurated in 2001, the championships have been held each year since, with the winner crowned "BASE Jumping World Champion." The events have been held in Malaysia, Russia, Germany, and Spain. At these major competitions, jumpers are evaluated on a number of safety-related criteria. The most "crowd-friendly" of these is accuracy in the landing area, as jumpers endeavor to hit a very small target as they come in to land. (Additional information on these championships can be located at http://www .thebasejump.com/ and http://www.johnnyutah.com/worldchampion shipstats.html, both accessed August 9, 2011.)

7. pioneers and icons

at the outset of this chapter, I should note that any list of "pioneers and icons" is likely (perhaps certain) to be partial, selective, and perhaps even biased. This one is no different. Though I have endeavored to include some of the most important and influential names in the history of BASE (and have had some of these jumpers endorse the list and offer their own suggestions), it remains a difficult task to decide who to profile and then to gather information shedding light on their lives and jumping careers. For example, names that could certainly have appeared on this list include Phil Smith and Phil Mayfield (BASE numbers 1 and 2, respectively; see Chapter 4); Jean Boenish (BASE number 4 and long-time organizer of Bridge Day); Erich Felbermayr and Wolfgang Weitzenböck (who jumped in the Italian Dolomites even earlier than Pelkey and Schubert jumped "El Cap"); Dwain Weston (who, prior to his death in October 2003, was thought to be perhaps the most "extreme" BASE jumper on the planet); Pete Fielding (sometimes referred to as the "Godfather of Australian BASE"). All of that said, I invite readers to learn a bit more about some of the biggest names in the sport, both from its early days and more recent years.

brian schubert (1940–2006)

Brian Schubert was born June 23, 1940, in Chicago, the eldest of four children. Schubert's mother was a beautician, and his father drove a Greyhound bus, though he later became an accountant. Before the birth of Schubert's two youngest siblings (twin sisters Karen and Karel), the family moved to Los Angeles, later settling in Claremont, California. Schubert was a smart child for whom school did not present much of a challenge. Schubert's first brush with death came at the age of 16, when he was stabbed by a friend during a (presumably heated) card game. The knife penetrated alarmingly close to his heart, but luckily Schubert came out of surgery relatively unscathed (Intini, 2006).

Before graduating from high school, Schubert joined the army. In the late 1950s, while stationed in Germany, his role as a paratrooper led to his passion for skydiving, which laid the foundation for his historic jump from El Capitan. After he returned home from army service, he married, and he and his wife had two children before divorcing. After the divorce, Schubert moved to Barstow, California, where he met Mike Pelkey. Schubert and Pelkey met as fellow 26-year-old skydivers, both of whom had an appetite for adventure. In the summer of 1966, Pelkey proposed to Schubert the idea of jumping from El Capitan in Yosemite National Park, and Schubert readily agreed. Pelkey later called him the "poster boy for fearlessness." About a month later, on July 24, 1966, they undertook this historic adventure. Jumping round parachutes, both men were, to some extent at least, at the whim of the wind conditions. Add to this the fact that there was no information available at the time about the specifics of jumping cliffs in general (and certainly not jumping "the Cap" in particular), and it is perhaps not surprising that both men suffered injuries as a result of the jump. Schubert's were the most severe, as he crashed hard into the talus. He told Pelkey that he had heard every bone in both feet break. Indeed, he walked with a limp for some time and was told by physicians that he would never walk properly again.

Unbeknownst to either of these men, this jump would inspire the first generation of jumpers who took the sport very seriously and, ultimately, created the acronym BASE. One of these jumpers, Carl Boenish, eventually acknowledged the importance of Pelkey and Schubert's accomplishment, issuing them certificates as El Capitan numbers 1 and 2, respectively.

Both Pelkey and Schubert were honored as guest speakers at the 26th annual Bridge Day event in Fayetteville, West Virginia, on October 15, 2005. Pelkey and Schubert planned to jump together at the 2006 Bridge Day event, a few months after the 40th anniversary of their first El Capitan jump. This jump never took place, as Schubert died on an individual jump, becoming the first participant to die at the Bridge Day festival since 1987.

michael pelkey (1940–)

Michael Pelkey, considered one of the pioneers of BASE jumping, was born on March 28, 1940, in St. Joseph, Michigan. He and Brian

Schubert jumped El Capitan on July 24, 1966, more than a decade before jumping in Yosemite National Park began in earnest.

Pelkey began skydiving in 1964, two years before jumping El Capitan. Asked later why he and Schubert decided to jump "the Cap," he said,

> It was more of a lark than a compulsion. Skydiving was a relatively new sport and the El Capitan was obviously jumpable, straight down 3,200 feet off the valley floor. If we hadn't got to it first, someone else inevitably would have. . . . We were two like-minded, somewhat adventurous 26-year-old sport parachutists who wanted to do something that hadn't been done before. The El Capitan was there and it had never been jumped.

Pelkey fractured his ankle after striking the cliff under canopy (in his opinion because he made the mistake of facing the cliff). Pelkey performed his second jump at Bridge Day in 2005 and was to have made his third in 2006 before Brian Schubert died.

Interestingly, before taking up cliff jumping, Pelkey at least dabbled with flying a gyroglider. With some college but no formal degree, Pelkey was an electronics and electromechanical design engineer. It was a picture of him on his gyroglider that appeared in a Benton Harbor, Michigan, newspaper on July 30, 1966, about his jump with Schubert. Considering the current popularity of BASE, it is somewhat ironic that in the article accompanying this photograph the reporter stated, "Mike Pelkey in 1964 thought his new gyrogliding plane would catch on like go-karting, but his newest venture—parachuting off a mountain probably won't have much success along similar lines" (Lutz 1966).

One of the elements of jumping an object for the first time, and particularly in a period when this was an uncommon undertaking, is that there is little helpful information available to guide the practical decisions jumpers have to make. In Pelkey's words,

> We got a few books from the library and studied what we could from them. The only real useful information we could glean was that the El Capitan was a sheer vertical monolith that rose 3,200 feet above the valley floor. Other rather important details such as wind patterns, landing areas, etc., had to be experienced empirically.
>   (http://www.basejumper.com/Articles/Interviews_and_Profiles/ Someone_You_Think_You_Know. . .15_Questions_with. . . Jeb_Corliss_855.html, accessed December 11, 2011)

It is often claimed that two things differentiated cliff jumping in the late 1970s from the jump of Schubert and Pelkey: rectangular parachutes and the ability to track. On the latter point, Pelkey once stated, "I laugh when I see the definition of 'modern' fixed object parachuting suggesting that tracking was a brand new invention. Imagine dropping off the top of a terminal object depending on luck to keep you from smashing into it on the way down. We knew how to track" (http://www.articlesbase.com/extreme-sports-articles/an-inspirational-first-base-jump-1249728.html, accessed March 25, 2012).

carl boenish (1941–1984)

Many consider Carl Boenish to be the "father" of BASE jumping. Though he was by no means the first to jump from a fixed object, he was one of the first to take seriously the idea of developing the sport into a form of recreation in which one could participate regularly. In this sense, Boenish was a visionary and exerted a significant influence on the early history of BASE (and, as an aside, the early history of hang-gliding). Born April 3, 1941, Boenish became an avid skydiver, beginning with his first

Californians Jean and Carl Boenish relaxing in Norway prior to filming a BASE jump in 1984. (AP/Wide World Photos)

jump in 1962 in Lake Elsinore, California. Eventually, Boenish became a prominent freefall cinematographer.

In the 1960s, Boenish was working as an electrical engineer for the Hughes Corporation. In 1966, he caught word that two jumpers from Barstow, California—Schubert and Pelkey—had jumped El Capitan. This jump planted the seed that eventually led to Boenish becoming perhaps the most important figure in the early history of modern BASE jumping.

Though Schubert and Pelkey's jump played some part in inspiring Boenish to jump from El Capitan, it was by no means the driving force. In part, this influence was limited by the fact that by the time Boenish decided to jump El Cap, Pelkey and Schubert had quit skydiving, so they were not available for consultation. However, Boenish consulted Rick Sylvester, a stuntman who parachuted from El Cap on skis in 1971 and 1972 (a feat that earned him notoriety and laid the foundation for some of his later Hollywood film work). In 1977, Boenish made a trip to Yosemite in order to film some hang-gliding footage. It was on this trip that he got to witness firsthand the nature of the cliffs in the park and to put the earlier jumps into perspective.

In 1978, Boenish documented a group that undertook several trips to research El Cap before eventually jumping it. On August 18, 1978, Kent Lane was the first member of this group to leap from the edge. Boenish was one of two men responsible for filming those first jumps, and he returned to El Cap on September 9 to jump it himself, along with five other jumpers.

In addition to spearheading many of the early BASE jumps and being a driving force behind developing BASE as a repeatable activity, Boenish published the first magazine devoted specifically to BASE: *BASE Magazine*. The magazine was published for a relatively brief period in the early 1980s with limited circulation. Online forums still abound with requests for original copies or electronic scans; however, these seem difficult to come by. At the time, however, the magazine allowed jumpers to share information with one another about objects, techniques, equipment, and so forth. Now, of course, the Internet is the main source of this kind of information.

Boenish's jumping career came to an end in June 1984. He and his wife Jean had been in Norway filming jumps for the *Guinness Book of World Records*. At the end of a week of filming, Boenish jumped from a new launch point and failed to clear a rocky outcropping in freefall, making him the first (but not the last) BASE fatality of the Trollveggen area. Three years after his death, Boenish was posthumously awarded a tremendous honor: the USPA Achievement Award.

anne helliwell (1959–)

Anne Helliwell, BASE number 222, is best known as the first person to develop a BASE-specific canopy. In the early 1980s, as BASE was in its infancy as an organized form of recreation, jumpers had little choice but to use skydiving canopies for their BASE jumps. For those "in the know," however, the requirements of skydiving and those of BASE are rather different. Considering the possibility of object strike, for example, and the tighter landing areas often associated with BASE jumping, it was acknowledged early on that a BASE-specific canopy that opened reliably and on-heading, was very stable in the air, and landed well even in deep brakes, was needed. Ultimately, it was Helliwell who first answered this need.

Helliwell had left her home in New Zealand in 1980 in order to pursue her passion of skydiving in the United States. She worked extensively as a rigger, manufacturing and repairing skydiving equipment. After taking up

Anne Helliwell, pioneer of BASE-specific parachute technologies. (AP/Wide World Photos)

BASE jumping in 1981, Helliwell—like other jumpers—recognized the need for a BASE canopy. In her case, however, she also realized that she had the expertise to build one. In 1985, Helliwell set out to build a BASE-specific canopy from scratch. Her prototype was called the "gray thing," and it both performed well in the field and established that there was, indeed, a market for such a product. Ultimately, Helliwell and Todd Shoebotham—who was manufacturing a Velcro-closing BASE container—joined forces to form the company Basic Research. The "gray thing" became the "Fox," the first BASE canopy that went to market and one that changed the face of the sport. Though the technology underlying the Fox might seem somewhat dated by today's standards, it laid the foundation upon which most, if not all, of today's BASE canopies are based.

In 2002, Anne decided to step back from manufacturing for a while, though she continued to jump. Eventually, she returned to join the Apex BASE team, which included her original partner Shoebotham as well as Marta Empinotti and Jimmy Pouchert. Once again, she became part of the vanguard of the industry and sport, not only helping develop cutting-edge technologies but also taking part in the instruction of new and junior jumpers as they developed their own skills in the sport.

In a 2002 interview, Helliwell spoke about the dangers of the sport and her understanding of how and why jumpers "crowd the edge," as Stephen Lyng would say: "We are all pushing the envelope. . . . Sometimes you get away with it and you win, sometimes you don't. But if you don't push the envelope, you don't advance and the sport doesn't advance" (http://www.basejumper.com/cgi-bin/forum/gforum.cgi?do=post_view_printable;post=304599;guest=2704860, accessed December 11, 2011).

patrick de gayardon (1960–1998)

Born in January 1960, Patrick de Gayardon is perhaps better known as a skydiver and skysurfer than as a BASE jumper (though he did all three). He might be best understood, though, as an innovator. He was a tremendously skilled skydiver and receives a good deal of (well-deserved) credit for inventing sky-surfing, a subdiscipline that was, for a time, quite popular, even making repeated appearances in the X Games. His constant push for innovation also led him to pursue the idea of a wingsuit with a passion and vigor that both drove him to excellence and, eventually, contributed to his untimely death. He was killed on a skydive in 1998 while testing a modification to his wingsuit design. Though he did not live long enough

French stuntman Patrick De Gayardon, wearing a wingsuit, flies over the Grand Canyon in 1998. (AP/Wide World Photos)

to witness the current proliferation of wingsuit jumping in both skydiving and BASE (and proximity flying in BASE), it is generally acknowledged that without the work he did in laying the foundation for this technology, current wingsuit technologies and skills would not be at their current levels.

marta empinotti (1964–)

Born in December 1964, one of her parents' four girls, Marta Empinotti is one of very few women in the elite echelon of BASE. She took up skydiving in Brazil in 1985 and only a year later, with less than 100 skydives under her belt, began her now iconic career in the sport of BASE, undertaking her first jump at the New River Gorge Bridge in West Virginia. Asked why she jumps, Empinotti noted, "Jumping gives me what nothing else can, the feeling of ultimate freedom" (http://www.bird-man.com/athletes/individuals/marta-empinotti/, accessed March 21, 2012.) Elsewhere, she has explained that she is addicted to the sport, feeling cooped up if she goes too long between jumps. As one of the few figures in BASE jumping

Brazilian Marta Empinotti steers her parachute during a 2004 jump in Kuala Lumpur. (AFP/Getty Images)

with some degree of celebrity beyond practitioners of the sport, Empinotti has been interviewed on numerous occasions. In a 1998 interview with *Sports Illustrated* (see http://sportsillustrated.cnn.com/vault/article/magazine/MAG1014686/index.htm, accessed December 11, 2011), she elaborated on the spiritual side of BASE jumping to which I have referred in Chapter 1:

> Most people look at a tower as just a pile of steel. . . . To me it is a thing of beauty, a piece of art. When I'm high above the ground, maybe six or eight hundred feet up, the feeling is very spiritual. I look down, and if there is fog, all I can see are the tips of the trees. On the horizon the sun is rising, turning the clouds pink and yellow. It's so peaceful; it's like paradise. I'm not impressing anyone, because nobody knows I'm there. It's just me and nature. Then I jump and feel the thrill. When I land, I see the sun rise again. How many people watch the sun rise twice in one day?

Though Empinotti clearly considers jumping to be a spiritual activity, she, like most seasoned jumpers, is also familiar with the darker side of the sport. In 1987, she was filming her then boyfriend when he experienced a malfunction, plunging to his death from the same bridge where Empinotti began her BASE career. Almost two decades later, after witnessing another fatality, Empinotti commented: "It's always devastating. . . . But as a jumper, you think, 'What's the option?' To live not fully? To be afraid of living? Because people like us—we need this" (http://www.usatoday.com/news/nation/2006-06-10-base-jumpers_x.htm, accessed March 21, 2012).

Empinotti is considered by many to be the most experienced female BASE jumper on the planet. She has appeared in numerous films, commercials, and television shows, including a memorable appearance on *Stunt Junkies*, doing a BASE jump from a moving semi trailer as it crossed the Foresthill Bridge in California.

In addition to her career as a jumper, Empinotti has made an indelible imprint on the sport as both a gear manufacturer and course instructor. She was one of the driving forces behind Vertigo BASE Outfitters, which later joined forces with key staff from Basic Rearch to become Apex BASE, recognized as an industry leader in manufacturing and providing equipment, organizing BASE expeditions, and consulting for commercials and films.

lonnie bissonnette (1965–)

Like many BASE jumpers, Bissonnette has a storied history in skydiving, having been an instructor for several years and then a highly successful competitive jumper, competing for Canada in formation skydiving at the world championships. He also spent some time as a "camera-flyer," employed to film other people's skydives. Later, he competed in the first world championships of BASE jumping in Malaysia.

Bissonnette may be best known in the BASE community for his passion and perseverance. His passion for BASE and for pushing various kinds of limits in the activity is perhaps best exemplified by a story he shares in Herminio Cordido's 2007 film *I'd Rather Fly*. In it, Bissonnette recounts that a number of jumpers were endeavoring to achieve a specialized BASE number not simply by jumping from objects in each of the four categories but by doing so naked. Not particularly interested in a naked BASE number, Bissonnette decided to push the envelope a bit further. He jumped from each of the objects in subzero temperatures, thereby qualifying for subzero naked BASE number 1. This passion, coupled with tremendous commitment to BASE, translates into being well regarded by other jumpers, including some of those profiled here. Chris McDougall, for instance, said about Bissonnette: "He . . . preserved his local sites better than anyone I know. . . . He is a . . . legend" (http://cynthialynn chronicles.com/2010/07/08/lonnie-bissonnette-interview-what-lies -within-us/, accessed March 21, 2012).

Like a number of jumpers on this list (and beyond), Bissonnette speaks of BASE jumping in general, and particular jumps more specifically, in terms that point to a spiritual attachment to the activity. For example, in a 2010 interview with Cynthia Lynn (see http://cynthialynnchronicles .com/2010/07/08/lonnie-bissonnette-interview-what-lies-within-us/, accessed December 11, 2011), he had this to say about a jump at Angel Falls in Venezuela: "That place called to me. I am so glad that I did that jump; you know the tallest waterfall in the world. Angel Falls was a magical place for me that held so much in a spiritually emotional way. The place spoke to me; it was so gorgeous and majestic."

Bissonnette is very clear to distinguish between the "right" and "wrong" reasons for being a BASE jumper. In the same interview, he stated,

I hope everyone I have taught is doing it because they love it and not because they think it's cool. . . . It's your life on the line. And if you are

Lonnie Bissonnette (right), competing at the Malaysia International Extreme Skydiving Championship in 2001. (AP/Wide World Photos)

doing it because you think it's cool, you are doing it for the wrong reasons. You really need to possess a passion and love for it. It's not about being cool, because it really isn't. I have met guys out there where BASE jumping is a cool card to them and not a passion.

This is not to suggest that Bissonnette doesn't get a "rush" from jumping. Quite the contrary, in fact: in that same interview, he described where that rush comes from, in his perspective. "I think it's placing yourself in uncomfortable positions that gives you the rush and challenge, or in situations where say, you are unfamiliar. . . . You know, I love to do things that people thought couldn't be done or that people had said, 'No you can't do that.'"

In July 2004, Bissonnette's BASE career changed dramatically. He was jumping with several other highly experienced BASE jumpers at the Perrine Bridge. He executed four backflips prior to deployment, as he had done numerous times before. This time, however, he became entangled with his parachute during the deployment sequence and, as a result, crashed into the ground at a tremendous speed (he essentially had no parachute at the time). He broke several ribs, his femur, and most importantly his back. About the jump, he later said, "Hindsight is always 20/20" (Cordido 2007). In light of the extent of his injuries, many people (fellow jumpers included) assumed that that this signaled an end to Bissonnette's jumping career. Bissonnette, however, adamantly insisted that he would continue to jump. His injuries have, of course, changed the *way* he jumps, but they did not end his jumping career. After a year away from BASE, he returned to the activity, jumping with his wheelchair (a story about Bissonnette and another member of a group known as "extreme chairing" jumping at the 2010 Bridge Day event can be found at http://www.extremechairing.com/news/2010/paralized%20base %20jumping.html, accessed August 9, 2011). Though Bissonnette adamantly rejects any hero status, he is deeply respected by other jumpers for his continued commitment to BASE following his spinal cord injury.

Bissonnette is reflective about his limitations with respect to BASE. In his interview with Cynthia Lynn, he stated,

Probably my biggest weakness would be that I was never satisfied. I always wanted to do more, go harder. I was never satisfied. When I first learned how to do aerials, one flip was cool, okay that's great and after doing a couple well now I wanted to a double, then a triple, and then I want to do flipping twisting aerial because flipping one direction wasn't enough anymore. I was never happy; I was never happy with what I had. I had to always push it. Unfortunately it can bite you in the ass too.

Bissonnette also worries about the new generation of jumpers for reasons hinted at in earlier chapters. Like other long-time jumpers, he is ambivalent about the ways in which new media technologies have shaped and are shaping the activity. In that same interview, he elaborated on this idea:

. . . my generation and guys who came up before me there wasn't all this video to show what other guys were doing. Unless you heard it by word of mouth, you didn't know. So you didn't know how badass Buddy was down in Cincinnati or Tracy back when he was down in Florida or Mark Hewitt, you didn't know, you didn't see it. You would hear stories about it, but you didn't actually visually see it. So, part of it is the younger generation and they do seem to want it now and don't want to wait and I think the other part is all the video that is out there now. There is so much video that people can see and its tempting people.

roland "slim" simpson (1969–2004)

Like many of the jumpers profiled here, Australian Roland Simpson was an accomplished skydiver before he got involved in BASE jumping, having completed numerous certifications and competed in (and won) multiple major championships. Simpson also served as the president of the Australian BASE Association for a time.

Simpson's BASE career was marked by both remarkable successes and tremendous tragedy. Simpson won a number of awards and made numerous noteworthy jumps, including leaps from the Petronas Twin Towers in Malaysia, Troll Wall in Norway, and the Cave of the Swallows in Mexico (see Chapter 6). Simpson also participated in a record jump for the largest formation BASE jump in July 2004, when 30 jumpers leapt at the same time from the Ostankino Radio Tower in Moscow, Russia. Simpson's skills and experience in BASE were well respected, as indicated by the fact that he was invited to be the technical director for the 2003–2004 World BASE Cup.

Roland Simpson (white shirt) jumping over Kuala Lumpur in 2001. (AP/Wide World Photos)

In a 2003 interview, Simpson described the overwhelming sensations associated with a jump:

> In that first second or two when you actually, when you're actually, when your body's hanging in the air and you're starting to drop and you look down and this enormous rock wall starts to race past and you're accelerating down right next to it, that visual impression that's this kaleidoscope of rock racing past you, is very difficult to explain. It's an incredible feeling—really amazing. (http://www.abc.net.au/radionational/programs/sportsfactor/sensational-the-reason-people -jump-out-of/3170918, accessed March 21, 2012)

In the same interview, Simpson acknowledged that participation in BASE can be quite tough on loved ones: "I think BASE jumping is really quite a selfish sport. It's very hard on family, I think it's hard on people who don't necessarily understand what it is that you're doing and it would seem ridiculous why you would take such risks just to have some fun." He described trying to "shelter" his family "by not really telling them a great deal of what I'm doing and it's more because I don't want them worrying or stressing or panicking about what I'm going to be doing this weekend or next weekend or whatever."

In April 2001, Simpson was badly injured on a jump. A year later, he was back in BASE, actively jumping for the remainder of his life. In October 2004, Simpson was part of an international group of jumpers invited by the Shanghai Sports Bureau to leap from the top of a tower in the financial district. The day following this jump, he did a wingsuit jump from the top of the tallest skyscraper in China. The launch and flight were uneventful, but his parachute malfunctioned, and he crashed into a nearby building. The crash put him in a coma from which he never recovered. He died of his injuries on October 22, 2004.

jeb corliss (1976–)

In terms of modern-day BASE jumping, Jeb Corliss is definitely an icon of the sport. He began jumping in 1997, but in a short time established a reputation as someone who was going to push limits—both his own and those of the sport itself. He has summed up his philosophy of jumping:

> For me B.A.S.E. jumping has been an exercise in learning to control fear. I have always felt you have two choices in life. You can either learn to control your fears or you can allow your fears to control you. B.A.S.E jumping helped me learn how to harness fear, confront fear and has made it much easier for me in my everyday life to deal with fear. After you have jumped off a few dozen buildings everything else seems less scary.
> (http://www.basejumper.com/Articles/Interviews_and_Profiles/ Someone_You_Think_You_Know. . .15_Questions_with. . .Jeb _Corliss_855.html, accessed March 21, 2012)

Corliss was born in March 1976, the middle of three children and the only boy. His parents traveled extensively throughout Corliss's early childhood, perhaps helping to instill in Corliss the adventurous spirit for which he is so famous. When Corliss was eight, his parents divorced and he, his mother, and his sisters settled in Palm Springs, California.

Corliss, like many other jumpers, understands BASE to be something much bigger than a sport: "For me B.A.S.E. jumping is a philosophy. It's an understanding of one's own mortality. It's about going out in the world and pushing the boundaries of what you can do. To call it a sport is to insult it. Sports are games with made up rules with little or no real consequences" (http://www.basejumper.com/Articles/Interviews_and_Profiles/Someone _You_Think_You_Know. . .15_Questions_with. . .Jeb_Corliss_855.html, accessed March 21, 2012). He sees BASE as something much more real, as a much better test of a person's mettle: "It becomes a journey into one's own mind. If you didn't know yourself before you started jumping, you will after you have done it long enough" (http://www.basejumper .com/Articles/Interviews_and_Profiles/Someone_You_Think_You_Know ...15_Questions_with...Jeb_Corliss_855.html, accessed March 21, 2012). BASE is not something Corliss does in his spare time—from his perspective, it is simply the reason he is on this earth. In a phone conversation, he mentioned that interviewers often ask him when he will give up the sport. That, he said, is akin to walking up to a bird and saying: "When are you gonna' stop this whole flying thing?"

Corliss is perhaps best known for what he has referred to as the "landing project." The project, one that promises to be an extremely costly one both in terms of time and money, is to land without a parachute. Corliss (and others, it should be noted) believe that it is possible to land a wingsuit without deploying one's parachute. The basic premise is that you can fly a wingsuit much like you would fly a parachute, approaching a landing area at just the right angle in order to land safely (more detail is provided in Chapter 8). This project has led some to question Corliss's motivations in the sport, suggesting that he is seeking glory. This does not trouble Corliss much, as he seems clear about his own motivations and unworried about what others will make of them:

> People are entitled to their opinions and are free to think whatever they like about me. I am just a person trying to live my life the best that I can. I am not perfect and I do make mistakes. I have dreams and all I am trying to do is turn them into realities. . . . I love showing people that the only limits are the ones we place upon ourselves. (http://www .basejumper.com/Articles/Interviews_and_Profiles/Someone _You_Think_You_Know. . .15_Questions_with. . .Jeb_Corliss_855 .html, accessed March 21, 2012)

chris "douggs" mcdougall (1976–)

Chris "Douggs" McDougall was born on April 17, 1976, the oldest of four children. He grew up with his parents and sisters in Keysborough, a suburb 27 km southeast of the central district of Melbourne, Australia. At the time of this writing, McDougall has over 1960 base jumps and almost 7,000 skydives to his credit, and he produces underground extreme BASE jumping videos as well. In 2009, he authored *Confessions of an Idiot*, providing both BASE jumpers and those simply interested in extreme sport an insight into his jumping and social exploits. McDougall was crowned the 2003–2004 world BASE jumping overall champion (see Chapter 6) and holds numerous other competitive titles.

In addition to his involvement in BASE, McDougall is a highly successful skydiver, qualified as both a tandem and AFF instructor and active as a camera and wingsuit flyer. He also participated in international skydiving competitions, representing Australia at the 2001 and 2003 world championships in eight-way formation skydiving, with his teams finishing fourth and sixth overall, respectively.

McDougall is something of a celebrity by BASE jumping standards, having been interviewed by numerous mainstream and alternative media outlets. In addition, he has appeared in numerous films, including *Journey to the Center*, a recent award-winning entry in the Banff Mountain Film Festival. The film documents McDougall's expedition (with Jeb Corliss and Paul Fortun) to jump Tian Keng, the "Heavenly Pit." As the film's website suggests, Tian Keng, near Chongqing, China, is "millions of years old, half a mile deep, waiting for eons to test the endurance, skill and courage of the men who dare to parachute into her heart." Some suggest that McDougall is the "rockstar" of BASE jumping, with others implying that he is the poster child for the renegade bad-boy element of BASE. There is undoubtedly a kernel of truth to these claims, as McDougall acknowledges in his book: "If you go and tell a BASE jumper that he shouldn't be doing something, he's going to tell you to get stuffed. That's the reason why he started the sport anyway, because there's no real rules in BASE jumping; there's just underlying etiquette." He is also, though, tremendously thoughtful about his participation in BASE, skydiving, and other adventure activities and about life more generally. He has fashioned his own approach to BASE, and to life more broadly, one for which he is sometimes criticized. And yet he seems crystal clear about his motives. In a 2010 radio interview, for example, he noted, "Quitting my job and becoming a professional skydiver was the best thing I've ever done in my life. It changed everything for the better, and it allowed me to break free from conventional society and travel the world, meeting new people, and seeing awesome places" (http://www.blogtalkradio.com/cynthialynnchronicles3/2010/05/21/australian-adventurer-chris-douggs-mcdougall, accessed March 21, 2012).

While the quote above might seem to suggest a hedonistic approach to life, in that same interview McDougall reflects deeply about what he sees as the disjunct between Western values and practices and the awareness he has gained from his travels and experiences of what is really important—the human condition. This belies the surface construction of a bad boy purely searching for his own pleasure. This surface construction, though, is perhaps understandable in that McDougall took a somewhat unconventional route as he negotiated the relationship between work and leisure. In the same interview, he describes his experiences of his early years in BASE: "I've slept on a lot of hard floors, I've slept on roads, and car-parks, and things like that, but, you know, my dream was to travel the world jumping, and I got to do that. . . . So, that's how you do it. You find your niche in life, and you have a passion for your dream, and you get there no matter what."

McDougall also demonstrates a seriousness about the hazards of the sport, one influenced by having lost a number of close friends in BASE and skydiving. He talks about the risk/reward ratio, acknowledging that the risks of the sport are great, so the rewards had better be or else you're not "in it" for the right reasons. In the radio interview quoted above, McDougall was asked how he reconciles his own promotion of the sport—through videos and his book, for example—with the perception held by some BASE jumpers that this kind of promotion is counterproductive because it encourages the idea that just about anyone can take up the sport. His reply:

I'm on both sides of the fence. A lot of the issues that you see on the BASE jumper websites and stuff, I agree and disagree with. . . . It's a double-edged sword, really, because having that knowledge out there for people to look at definitely saves lives, but also gives people an opportunity to do it that probably shouldn't be doing it. When I learned to BASE jump, we really made it up ourselves [in contrast to now]. The hard part of BASE jumping is that it is extremely dangerous if you don't do it properly.

8. future directions

BASE is perhaps the archetype of what sociologist Stephen Lyng (1990; 2005) calls edgework. In these kinds of activities, Lyng (1990, 855) claims, participants use both technical skill and the ability to remain calm in the face of danger in order to "negotiate the boundary between chaos and order." It is not the case, Lyng and others have pointed out, that edge-workers have a death wish, as is often suggested by nonparticipants— quite the opposite, in fact. The point of these activities is not to put oneself in harm's way but to wander as far out on the "edge" as possible *while still maintaining control.* Other researchers, for example, have called BASE "the most serious play in the world," emphasizing the time and energy jumpers devote to maintaining their safety in the sport (Martha and Griffet 2006). This does not mean, of course, taking as few risks as possible. Jumpers determine the kinds of jumps they are capable of doing, the conditions under which they are capable of doing them, and then generally do everything possible to make sure that the jump is repeatable.

A number of new technologies and controversies promise to shape both the future of the activity itself and the possibilities for research into participation in this extreme sport. In terms of research, anecdotal evidence points to the possibility that BASE jumpers (like some other extreme sport enthusiasts) might not be inclined to talk in depth with researchers investigating BASE jumping from a social-scientific perspective. I have not encountered this problem myself, but that is likely shaped in part by my connections (through skydiving) to a number of jumpers and the fact that I was an active participant in the activity for a short time, (thus marking me as an insider). The worry seems to be that an outsider may paint an unflattering (and, from the perspective of an active participant, unfair) picture of the activity, perhaps even without intending to do so. A number of jumpers with whom I spoke relaxed noticeably when we talked about my own participation in skydiving and BASE, and I understood this as an indication that they worried less that I might misrepresent them and the sport because I was likely to understand it better (from their vantage point, at least).

Overall, the hazards of BASE, together with the fact that jumpers occasionally engage in illegal activities as part of undertaking their jumps, will make the process of conducting research into the activity a daunting one. At the same time, however, this is part of what marks BASE as an intriguing activity to consider from a sociological perspective.

In terms of the activity itself, advances in equipment and human performance will almost certainly continue to expand the possibilities of what BASE jumpers can do in their activity. The wingsuit discussed in Chapter 5, for example, is setting the stage for the most cutting-edge activities in BASE. Increasingly BASE jumpers are jumping from cliffs and "flying" just a few meters from the trees and rock using wingsuits, following the slope of a cliff as it descends, before deploying their parachutes. Proximity flying is a spectacular activity, footage of which is increasingly made available to everyone via YouTube or other video-sharing technologies. One worry that some jumpers (particularly those who have been in the sport for some time) have is that the visibility of these jumps at the cutting edge will make the sport more dangerous for less experienced jumpers. They worry that newer jumpers do not necessarily have the skill or judgment to carry off proximity flying with a necessary degree of safety, yet they might be more likely to take it up prematurely because they so often see it in video format, if not in person. Whether or not this scenario is playing out, or is likely to do so, would be a fruitful avenue for investigation.

Another dimension to BASE that bears emphasizing at this point is the crossover between various extreme sports. A number of my contacts, for example, engage in "ski- or snowboard-BASE," launching from an object (generally a cliff) by literally skiing or snowboarding off of the edge. In certain respects, this is not so different from early pioneers riding bicycles (for example) off El Capitan as a way of making their jumps more interesting. However, when these activities are combined in ways that demand high levels of technical ability in more than one activity (keeping in mind that such ability takes years to develop in just one such undertaking), this increases the potential for things to go awry. The recent experience of noted Canadian-born skier and BASE jumper Shane McConkey is a case in point. McConkey, a highly accomplished and acclaimed ski racer and extreme skier, was also a pioneer of ski-BASE and became famous for such feats as jumping from "the Eiger." His prowess in these activities led to appearances in over 20 films, including *Steep*, a 2007 documentary that grossed over a quarter of a million U.S. dollars. In March 2009, McConkey died undertaking a highly technical ski-BASE jump during the shooting of a Red Bull commercial in Italy. One of McConkey's skis failed to release, sending him into a high-speed spin, thus leaving him unable to deploy his parachute before impact with the ground.

It is tremendously difficult to predict the future of a sport like BASE because the only limitations are the imaginations of those who are pushing the boundaries and the physical and technical abilities to bring these imaginations to reality. For example, as this book was nearing completion, a BASE contact posted a link to a video of jumpers undertaking what he called "tethered wingsuit jumps." In this video, jumpers were exiting from a cliff and had what appeared to be a bungee cord attached to them as they did so. The bungee was quite lengthy and seemed to be anchored to a point strung between adjacent cliffs, so that when jumpers reached the end of the tether they did not simply recoil into the cliff from which they had just jumped. Instead, after several seconds of freefall, they simply get suspended, having done a BASE jump without a parachute, which, of course, raises the question of whether or not this constitutes a BASE jump.

Jeb Corliss's landing project (introduced in Chapter 7) is currently the cutting edge in BASE and illustrates the idea outlined above rather well. Corliss firmly believes that someone will land without a parachute in the next couple of years. It is clear from talking with Corliss that this is not an ego project. First, he is fundamentally interested in this project as part of a broader search for what we as humans are capable of. Second, he does not suggest for a moment that he's the only jumper who has the skill to carry this off. In fact, he says that though the average person, the average skydiver, or even the average BASE jumper would be killed trying to do this, the average wingsuit flyer, who has been doing proximity flying for a few years, has the technical skill to undertake this feat. There are 40 or 50 people in the world, he suggests, who could do it and who will be lining up to try it out as soon as someone pulls it off. What's more, he points out, it is essentially already being done. The sport of ski-jumping, Corliss argues, is based on the same basic principles as landing a wingsuit in BASE. From the highest jumps especially (what's sometimes known as ski-flying), jumpers are in the air for several seconds—long enough to approach terminal velocity. The main difference between that and landing a wingsuit, in Corliss' view, is that ski-jumpers maintain a consistent

The Eiger, located in the Bernese Alps in Switzerland, peaks at nearly 4,000 m and is a touchstone of sorts in the rock-climbing community. For a time (in the early twentieth century), it had a reputation as "unclimbable," and a number of historical and fictional works have dramatized attempts (often ending in tragedy) at reaching its peak. Perhaps most famously, Clint Eastwood directed and starred in the 1975 film *The Eiger Sanction*, which grossed approximately $14 million. (Manfred Thuerig/Dreamstime.com)

Jeb Corliss undertaking a wingsuit BASE jump in September 2011. (Getty Images)

angle of descent throughout their jumps, whereas BASE jumpers have to "find" the right angle in order to land safely. Because a BASE jumper "exits" from higher altitudes, he or she must transition between falling more or less straight down on exit to the angle of approach needed in order to land safely. The point, Corliss says, is that landing without a parachute is already being done; what he and others are doing, simply, is to take that to the next level by doing so without the aid of a ski-jump and skis. The limiting factor in realizing this goal, he says, is not technical skill but funding. The technology to land a wingsuit is already in place. What is expensive, he notes, is the technology to make it possible to abort a landing if the approach is unsatisfactory in order to do a go-around for another approach (much like an airplane would do) and the technology to make sure that when a jumper lands with a tremendous amount of speed he or she is not hurt in the process. The sheer expense of this kind of technology, combined with the risks (or perceived risks) when something like this is undertaken for the first time, have been prohibitive and have stretched the timeline out well beyond what Corliss originally predicted. Nevertheless, his resolve is unshaken. "I'll do this," he says, "or I'll die trying." This kind of project illustrates both the ingenuity and imagination that it takes to be at the leading edge of any sport, but especially one like

BASE. In an interview with Cyntia Lynn, Corliss says, "This has become an obsession for me. I will do whatever it takes to make this project come to fruition. It's a complex puzzle in figuring out how to do something that has never been done before. It's really what I live for now" (http://www .basejumper.com/Articles/Interviews_and_Profiles/Someone_You _Think_You_Know ... 15_Questions_with ... Jeb_Corliss_855. html, accessed March 21, 2012). It also, though, points to the controversy that can be generated when someone is undertaking a project with such high potential to go badly, for what some think is no good reason. Corliss firmly disagrees, drawing a parallel between the landing project and the first summit of Mount Everest. Neither is likely to change anything, but both are clear illustrations of what humans can do if they put their heart and soul into a project.

The BASE jumping industry also presents a number of possible research questions to be explored. As I have documented throughout this book, there has been a notable shift over the past two decades towards an increasingly rational approach to BASE. In the early years (of the modern era, at least), almost all jumpers were highly experienced sky-divers who knew their gear extremely well, and jumpers shared informa-tion horizontally. For some time, basically the only way to get into BASE was to do so with the support of a mentor already involved in the activity. Increasingly, it is possible to take up BASE with relatively little skydiving experience and to do so without necessarily having the kind of mentoring I refer to. This is possible through the kinds of courses offered by manufacturers and instructors. And while these courses generally con-tain very good information, some jumpers fear that they are not an adequate substitute for long-term mentorship—only so much guidance (technical, emotional, social) can be passed along in 4, or even 10, days. Moreover, this speaks to something of a trend towards BASE becoming available as a bit of a thrill ride, something akin to a white-water rafting adventure where one pays for an expert to expose him or her to the activity while taking care of the risk management. Perhaps the clearest sign that this may be on the horizon is the recent arrival of BASE tandem. As of the time of this writing, one company (located in Twin Falls, Idaho) offers a service, available to anyone over 18 years of age, regardless of their experience (or lack thereof) in skydiving, to do a BASE jump.

Analogous to a BASE jump in skydiving, a tandem BASE jump involves a student doing a jump while attached to an instructor via a har-ness. The student and instructor jump and land together, suspended by one parachute designed to hold the weight of both jumpers. This new service points towards both the commodification of BASE as a thrill ride of sorts as well as a new entry point into the activity. Tandem BASE (the company's name) is careful to point out on their website that students "will have entered the world of base with [their] first base jump. Just as in skydiving, a single tandem does not prepare you for solo jumping, but is a start to whatever path you decide to take in jumping" (http://tandembase.com/faq, accessed March 21, 2012). Students are invited to request further information about training beyond the initial jump from Tandem BASE instructors. While this disclaimer is an important one, the implicit message seems to be that one can enter into the sport of BASE without much (if any) skydiving experience. Presumably, instructors would insist on a baseline level of experience in skydiving (or perhaps paragliding) before approving a student for further training. Nevertheless, it will be interesting to see both how this plays out "on the ground" and how the jumping community more broadly responds to this kind of service provision.

At the end of the day, there is something deeply seductive about stepping to the "edge," scared beyond belief, and pushing yourself to jump anyway. As the activity develops, we will continue, I strongly suspect, to see BASE grow on two fronts. On one, more people will become involved in the sport, with or without what some jumpers would consider the appropriate preparation. On the other, experienced jumpers will continue to push the boundaries of the activity in the seemingly never-ending search for the limits of human performance. Both of these potential trends have the potential, indeed are almost certain, to result in serious injuries and death. As social scientists, we have the opportunity to continue to delve into what it is that makes the "payoff" worth it for practitioners in activities like BASE and to consider the sociocultural context within which BASE and other extreme sports proliferate.

glossary

aerials.   The term aerials refers to a jumper performing flips on exit. The most straightforward jumps involve exiting with chest and head high, remaining flat and stable for a length of time, and then deploying one's parachute. For more advanced and daring jumpers, though, this may be considered a bit boring (depending on the object, wind conditions, etc.). For them, doing aerials might make a jump more interesting.

BASE ethics.   BASE ethics refers to two main ideas. The first is that jumpers are expected to have as little impact on the object and environment as possible, as captured in the phrase "take nothing but photographs, leave nothing but footprints." The second element of BASE ethics is the expectation that jumpers undertake the activity in such a way as not to impinge on the activities of other jumpers. This includes, for example, the expectation that one contacts local jumpers in a new city in order to determine whether there are particular protocols around certain objects.

Brakes.   When a jumper pulls on the steering lines, the canopy is said to be in brakes (on a steep landing approach, for example, a jumper might approach in "half brakes"). The brakes are also set during a pack job. The steering lines are secured in such a way that the canopy opens with the brakes set (to a greater or lesser extent), in part to minimize the amount of forward drive the canopy has initially. This is a safety measure—in the event of an off-heading opening, a jumper would have more time to engage in evasive maneuvers of some kind before object strike.

Bridle.   A bridle is a piece of material that links the pilot chute to the upper surface of the parachute. During the deployment sequence, it is the bridle (pulled by the drag created by the pilot chute) that both opens the container and extracts the suspension lines and parachute.

Burnt object. This term refers to a case where someone has jumped an object in such a way as to bring attention to it—especially the attention of the authorities. This brings "heat" on the object, compromising the ability of other jumpers to jump the same object without getting caught. This is considered a violation of BASE ethics.

Canopy. A canopy is the parachute itself. In modern BASE jumping, most canopies are rectangular in terms of their basic shape and are designed with the principles of airplane-wing technology in mind.

Cells. Modern BASE canopies are comprised of a number of cells (usually seven) open at the front (nose) of the canopy and closed at the back (tail).

Current. A current jumper is one who has done a number of jumps recently. The idea is that when one is current, one is better practiced both with the generalities of BASE jumping and with particular kinds of jumps. One can be current on particular kinds of jumps as well as BASE jumping itself.

Delay. A delay is the amount of time a jumper spends in freefall between exiting and pulling, and is a function of the nature of the object as well as a jumper's comfort level with the particular jump.

Drop zone. A facility for sport parachuting operations, with one or more designated landing areas. In most areas, drop zones are licensed by, and fall under the supervision of, a federal body such as the Federal Aviation Administration in the United States. Informally, day-to-day operations are managed by an individual or group managing the safety of the operation, generally in accordance with the safety rules and recommendations of a sport parachuting body such as the United States Parachute Association.

Exit. Used by jumpers as a verb, to exit means to launch from an object. It may also be used to describe the chosen spot to exit from an object. In some cases, a particular object (e.g., a cliff) may have numerous exits (sometimes called exit points). Whether a particular spot constitutes a good exit point is a function of a number of elements, including wind strength and direction (particularly in the case of an antenna), the features of the object (e.g., whether a cliff face is overhung or not), and, in some cases, considerations associated with being caught (e.g., whether the exit would draw more or less attention to an illegal jump). Certain exit points are known to involve a greater potential hazard than others, generally speaking. For example, at the Perrine Bridge in Twin Falls, Idaho, jumping from the side of the bridge further from the landing area is informally referred to as jumping from the "dark side." (The distance to the preferred landing area is greater from this side, with many more hazards along the way.)

Flare. To flare, a jumper pulls on the left and right toggles at the same time and with equal pressure. The result is that the tail of the canopy on both sides is somewhat cupped, converting the canopy's forward speed to lift and drag. The result, if it is properly performed, is a soft, safe landing.

Go and throw. A go and throw is when a jumper exits with her or his pilot chute already in hand and throws the pilot chute in the first second or two as they fall away. One does this from an object that is too low for a lengthier freefall delay but not so low that a static line or pilot-chute assist is called for.

Harness/container system. This is the part of a rig worn by a jumper; it is what connects a jumper to his or her parachute. It is composed of a harness worn by the jumper and a container in which the not-yet-deployed parachute is packed and contained.

Landing zone. An area that is formally or informally designated as the preferred landing area for a BASE jump.

Line-over. A line-over is a malfunction that can occur if, during a deployment sequence, there is slack in the suspension lines as a canopy is inflating. In the event that any part of a canopy inflates while suspension lines (usually steering lines) are over the top of the canopy, it is possible to have a line-over, the result of which is that part of the canopy is not fully inflated. In skydiving, this is not considered a major problem, both as it is less likely to occur (due to faster deployment sequences, as jumpers are generally at terminal velocity when they pull) and as the consequences are not as great because skydivers deploy much higher and hence have more time to deal with a malfunction. In BASE, a line-over could lead to a very hard landing, in the case of low objects, or, perhaps even worse, object strike. Because of the potential gravity of this situation, one common component of a BASE pack job is a tailgate (see Chapter 5).

Nose. This is the leading edge of the canopy and the opening of the cells.

Object.   Object is the general term for the fixed object from which a jumper exits.

Object strike.   Object strike involves flying into the object from which one has just jumped; for many jumpers, object strike represents the greatest hazard of BASE. Object strike may occur in freefall (as in the case of Carl Boenish, considered by some to be the "father" of modern BASE jumping) or under canopy. In freefall, object strike can occur if a jumper fails to clear a cliff outcropping, for example. Under canopy, there are more ways object strike can occur. Though it is not a common occurrence, it can happen in the case of unfavorable winds (most jumpers endeavor to avoid jumping in these conditions) or, more often, in the case of an off-heading opening. If, for example, a jumper's canopy opened facing backwards, the forward surge it would generate during the opening sequence would fly the jumper back toward the object from which he or she had just jumped. Object strike is more of a concern on some objects (e.g., buildings, cliffs) than others, as certain objects (the Perrine Bridge, for example) are constructed in such a way that jumpers generally have clear air around them during the opening sequence, making object strike extremely unlikely. The hazard in the case of object strike is that in addition to the potential harm caused by striking an object, this has the potential to have a negative effect on the flight characteristics of the parachute as well. This may result in a hard landing, landing in an unfavorable area, or, in the worst possible case, the result may be that the canopy deflates, returning the jumper to freefall and likely resulting in serious injury or death.

Opening.   This term refers to the overall opening sequence on a particular jump and especially to the speed of the opening and whether or not it is on heading. The speed is relevant both in terms of safety (one needs a faster opening on a jump from a lower object) and in terms of comfort (a "hard"—fast—opening can be quite uncomfortable, especially on a longer delay). Whether an opening is on heading is almost exclusively a safety issue. On-heading openings are extremely important in BASE, especially in terms of avoiding objects strike. Even if object strike does not occur, though, an off-heading opening can eat up altitude and may make it less likely that a jumper will reach the intended landing zone.

Out.   Jumpers use the term out to denote a backup plan to the designated landing zone. At Bridge Day, for example, the river is a suitable out in the event that a jumper does not feel that she or he will have a safe landing in the landing zone.

Pack job.   This refers to the finished product when one has packed the parachute, lines, and other equipment into their container.

Pilot chute.   A pilot chute is essentially a drogue. On most jumps (if one is not doing a static line or PCA), a jumper throws her or his pilot chute, which then creates drag, opens the container, and initiates the opening sequence.

Pilot-chute assist (PCA).   The idea behind a pilot-chute assist is to get a parachute deployed quickly. In the case of a PCA, another person is responsible for one's parachute opening quickly, as opposed to a static line, which an individual could rig up him- or herself. In a PCA situation, one person remains on the object, holding onto a second person's pilot chute while the second person falls away. The result is that the container is open quickly and the parachute is extracted quickly as well. This technique is commonly employed with newer jumpers, where a more experienced jumper will PCA them (used as a verb) so that they have less to worry about on their jump.

Proximity flying.   This is a relatively recent dimension of BASE jumping and may represent the cutting edge of the sport. Jumpers wear wingsuits and "fly" within feet (even inches) of objects such as cliff faces, bridges, and tree tops. The consequences of misjudgments in proximity flying are, of course, extreme.

Pulling.   This is a term used by jumpers for beginning the deployment sequence, usually by throwing their pilot chute.

Rig.   Rig is the term generally used to denote the combination of a harness/container system and a canopy.

Risers.   Risers are lengths of webbing that attach the container/harness system to the suspension lines. They are also important in terms of avoiding potential obstacles. Upon opening, jumpers are able to maneuver their canopy more quickly with risers than if they were to unstow the brakes first and then use their steering lines. The canopy also responds differently to riser input than to steering line input, meaning that risers are more appropriate for certain kinds of evasive maneuvers.

Runner.   A runner is a jump requiring a running launch. It takes somewhat more skill and practice to launch on heading on a runner than from
a standing position.

Slider.   The slider is a piece of material that has four rings through
which the suspension lines run. It can move along the suspension lines
and is principally used to slow the deployment sequence in the case of
jumps with slightly longer delays. As such, jumpers refer to "slider-up"
or "slider-down" jumps, depending on the nature of the object and the
delay they are planning.

Static line.   Like a PCA, a static line is a deployment method that is used
on low jumps when a jumper wants her or his parachute to be open as
quickly as possible. This method involves anchoring one's bridle to the
object (this may be as simple as wrapping some tape around it or may
involve a minor modification to the bridle itself) so that as a jumper falls
away from the object, the anchor pulls on the bridle, opening the container
and initiating the deployment sequence.

Steering lines.   Steering lines are the suspension lines that run to the
outer portions of the tail of the canopy. A jumper controls them with toggles, pulling on the left toggle, for example, in order to turn left, or on both
toggles simultaneously and evenly in order to flare for landing.

Suspension lines.   Suspension lines are the lines that run from the risers
to the canopy. Quite literally, they suspend a jumper from her or his canopy and also enable a jumper to steer the canopy, flare it for landing,
and perform other maneuvers. In an ideal deployment sequence, suspension lines are extracted from the container prior to the canopy being
extracted.

Tail.   The tail is the trailing edge of the canopy and is important for
steering and landing (see *Brakes* and *Flare*).

Tailgate.   A tailgate involves securing certain suspension lines to the tail
of the canopy during the pack job. The idea is that this forces the canopy
to inflate nose first, forcing any lines that may be above the canopy's top
surface away as the canopy inflates. It is generally agreed that this has
reduced the number of line-over malfunctions and hence improved the
safety of the sport.

Tandem.   A tandem is a parachute jump involving two people sharing one set of parachuting equipment. Though this has become commonplace in skydiving, only very recently has it made an appearance in BASE (see Chapter 8).

Terminal velocity.   Terminal velocity is the maximum vertical velocity in freefall, the point at which no further acceleration takes place due to the drag created by body position and equipment (e.g., a wingsuit). It can take up to 12 seconds of acceleration to reach terminal velocity, so for many BASE jumps it is not a factor. Without a wingsuit, terminal velocity for a flat, stable body position is somewhere around 120 mph (or 200 km/h).

Toggles.   Toggles are handles that are attached to the steering lines. When a rig is packed, the brakes are stowed, and the toggles secured to the risers. Once a jumper has confirmed that the canopy is open and flying well, he or she unstows the brakes by grabbing the toggles and pulling them down, releasing the extra length of steering line. This returns the canopy to full flight.

Tracking.   In order to track, a jumper extends her or his legs, sweeps her or his arms back, and de-arches slightly. The combined effect of this is to slow the jumper's fall rate slightly and to create forward speed. This is used to create separation between a jumper and the object from which he or she just exited. As it takes at least a few seconds to generate enough downward speed to track effectively, one does not often see tracking on objects involving a shorter delay.

Wingsuit.   A suit worn by a skydiver or BASE jumper in order to slow her or his vertical speed while increasing her or his ability to generate horizontal speed. Wingsuits are increasingly being used in cutting-edge practices in the sport, especially proximity flying.

bibliography

Adams, C. (2008). "Queens of the ice lanes": The Preston Rivulettes and women's hockey in Canada, 1931–1940. *Sport History Review, 39,1,* 1–29.

Allman, T., R. Mittelstaedt, B. Martin, and M. Goldenberg (2009). Exploring the motivations of BASE jumpers: Extreme sports enthusiasts. *Journal of Sport and Tourism, 14,4,* 229–247.

Anderson, L. (2011). Time is of the essence: An analytic autoethnography of family, work and serious leisure. *Symbolic Interaction, 34,2,* 133–157.

Beal, B. (1996). Alternative masculinity and its effects on gender relations in the subculture of skateboarding. *Journal of Sport Behavior, 19,3,* 204–220.

Beck, U. (1992). *Risk Society: Towards a New Modernity.* Thousand Oaks, CA: Sage.

Cooper, J., and J. Laurendeau. (2007). "BASE jumping." In D. Booth and H. Thorpe (eds.), *Berkshire Encyclopedia of Extreme Sports* (pp. 20–26). Great Barrington, MA: Berkshire Publishing Group.

Cordido, H. (Director, 2007). *I'd Rather Fly.* http://exposureroom.com/members/herminiocordido/2a093e5082d4437bad204e9f57277ef0/.

Crosset, T., and B. Beal (1997). The use of "subculture" and "subworld" in ethnographic works on sport: A discussion of definitional distinctions. *Sociology of Sport Journal, 14,1,* 73–85.

Donnelly, P. (2004). Sport and risk culture. In K. Young (ed.), *Sporting Bodies, Damaged Selves: Sociological Studies of Sports-related Injuries* (pp. 29–57). Oxford, UK: Elsevier.

Ferrell, J., D. Milovanovic, and S. Lyng (2001). Edgework, media practices, and the elongation of meaning: A theoretical ethnography of the Bridge Day event. *Theoretical Criminology, 5,2,* 177–202.

Hoffman, J. (Director, 2010). *Twenty Seconds of Joy.* F24 Film.

125

Hoffman, J. (Director, 2008). *Journey to the Centre.* Ground Impact, Inc.

Hunt, J. (1995). Divers' accounts of normal risk. *Symbolic Interaction, 18,4,* 439–462.

Hurt, Harry III. (1981). The ground's the limit. *Texas Monthly, 9,12,* 178–183; 293–304; 310. http://books.google.ca/books?id=3iwEAA AAMBAJ&pg=PA300&lpg=PA300&dq=base+magazine+boenish &source=bl&ots=RyJh_rQFem&sig=WMlpQ6lVFvA VKUuP1L SKdErPy8A&hl=en&ei=PQ6yTN2cMZ_zngfi8r3tBw&sa=X&oi =book_result&ct=result&resnum=4&ved=0CCQQ6AEwAw#v =onepage&q=base%20magazine%20boenish&f=true (accessed October 10, 2010).

Laurendeau, J. (2006). "He didn't go in doing a skydive": Sustaining the "illusion" of control in an edgework activity. *Sociological Perspectives, 49,4,* 583–605.

Laurendeau, J. (2008). "Gendered risk regimes": A theoretical consideration of edgework and gender. *Sociology of Sport Journal, 25,3,* 293–309.

Laurendeau, J. (2011). "If you're reading this, it's because I've died": Masculinity and relational risk in BASE jumping. *Sociology of Sport Journal, 28,4,* 404–420.

Laurendeau, J., and E. Gibbs Van Brunschot (2006). Policing the edge: Risk and social control in skydiving. *Deviant Behavior, 27,2,* 173–201.

Lienhard, J. (2006). *How Invention Begins: Echoes of Old Voices in the Rise of New Machines.* London: Oxford University Press.

Lupton, D. (1999). *Risk.* New York: Routledge.

Lutz, R. (1966). Former B.H. resident tries parachuting—without plane. *News-Palladium* (Benton Harbor, MI), July 30, 1966, 3.

Lyng, S. (1990). Edgework: A social psychological analysis of voluntary risk-taking. *American Journal of Sociology, 95,4,* 851–886.

Lyng, S. (2005). *Edgework: The Sociology of Risk-Taking.* New York: Routledge.

Martha, Cécile, and Jean Griffet (2006). Le BASE-jump, le jeu le plus sérieux du monde [BASE-jumping: The most serious play in the world]. *Ethnologie Française, 36,4,* 635–642.

McDermott, L. (2007). Governmental analysis of children "at risk" in a world of physical activity and obesity epidemics. *Sociology of Sport Journal, 24,3,* 302–324.

Monasterio, E. and O. Mei-Dan (2008). Risk and severity of injury in a population of BASE jumpers. *The New Zealand Medical Journal, 121,1277,* 70–75.

Olstead, R. (2011). Gender, space and fear: A study of women's edge-work. *Emotion, Space and Society, 4,2,* 86–94.

Palmer, C. (2002). "Shit happens": The selling of risk in extreme sport. *Australian Journal of Anthropology, 13,3,* 323–336.

"Parachute Leap off Statue of Liberty." (*New York Times*, February 12, 1912). http://query.nytimes.com/mem/archive-free/pdf?res =9B03E7DA173CE633A25750C0A9649C946396D6CF (accessed October 11, 2010).

Robinson, A., and C. Patrick (2008). The physics of Colonel Kittinger's longest lonely leap. *Physics Education, 43,5,* 477–482.

Rough, B. (2006/2007). The birdmen. *The Iowa Review, 36,3,* 27–40.

Soden, G. (2005). *Defying Gravity: Land Divers, Roller Coasters, Gravity Bums, and the Human Obsession with Falling.* New York: W.W. Norton.

Soreide, K., C. Ellingsen, and V. Knutson (2007). How dangerous is BASE jumping? An analysis of adverse events in 20,850 jumps from the Kjerag Massif, Norway. *Journal of Trauma—Injury Infection & Critical Care, 62,5,* 1113–1117.

Stebbins, R. (2007). *Serious Leisure.* New Brunswick, NJ: Transaction Publishers.

Svec, J. (December 1980). The shortest season. *Parachutist,* 37–42.

Taylor, J. (2010). *Pilgrims of the Vertical: Yosemite Rock Climbers and Nature at Risk.* Boston: Harvard University Press.

Westman, A., M. Rosén, P. Berggren and U. Björnstig (2008). Parachuting from fixed objects: Descriptive study of 106 fatal events in BASE jumping 1981–2006. *British Journal of Sports Medicine, 42,* 431–436.

Wheaton, B. (2004). *Understanding Lifestyle Sports: Consumption, Identity and Difference.* New York: Routledge.

White, L. (1978). *Medieval Religion and Technology: Collected Essays.* Berkeley: University of California Press.

Wood, R. (2003). The straightedge youth culture: Observations on the complexity of subcultural identity. *Journal of Youth Studies, 6,1,* 33–52.

index

about the author

JASON LAURENDEAU is an associate professor in the Department of Sociology at the University of Lethbridge in Lethbridge, Alberta, Canada. His research and teaching interests include risk, sport, and qualitative research methods.